A GUIDE FOR THE NEW NOVELIST

advice and common sense for the fiction writer

"Who wants to become a writer? And why? Because it's the answer to everything. ... It's the streaming reason for living. To note, to pin down, to build up, to create, to be astonished at nothing, to cherish the oddities, to let nothing go down the drain, to make something, to make a great flower out of life, even if it's a cactus."

—Enid Bagnold

LAURENT BOULANGER is an author of crime fiction and literary novels. His books have won awards in many countries, including the 2014 Paris Book Festival Award for Best Ebook and the eLit Award for Best Multicultural Fiction for his novel *The Girl From France*. His crime novel *Better Dead Than Never* was shortlisted for the CWAA's Best First Crime Novel and won a 2014 eLit Bronze Award for Best Multicultural Fiction. *First Kill* won a Tom Howard Mystery Novel Contest Honourable Mention. He has a Ph.D. in Writing and teaches creative writing at Swinburne University, Australia.

WINNER 2015 NEW ENGLAND BOOK FESTIVAL BEST HOW-TO
HONORABLE MENTION

by the same author

Literature
The Research
The Suffering
Addiction
The Girl From France

Crime
First Kill
Second Cut
Third Victim

Suspense
The Intern

Screenplay
Six Lovers
La Souffrance

A GUIDE FOR THE NEW NOVELIST

*advice and common sense
for the fiction writer*

LAKE OZARK PRESS

Lake Ozark Press

Copyright © 2018 Laurent Boulanger

All right reserved. No part of this book may be used or reproduced in any manner whatsoever without written permission except in the case of brief quotations embodied in critical articles and reviews.

Lake Ozark Press, Missouri, USA

Typeset in Garamond

Cover design © 2018 Lake Ozark Press

For Mike Slusher

A GUIDE FOR THE NEW NOVELIST

advice and common sense for the fiction writer

TO THE WRITER

"Writing a book is a horrible, exhausting struggle, like a long bout of some painful illness. One would never undertake such a thing if one were not driven on by some demon whom one can neither resist nor understand."

—George Orwell

I have been writing for as long as I can remember. At the age of thirteen I fell in love with books and spent hours reading and escaping into worlds of fiction. It was only natural that I would eventually want to write books myself. To date I have published nine novels, both crime fiction and literary fiction, commercially published and small-press published, with several of them winning international awards in several categories in the USA, Europe and Australia for best fiction, best e-book and best sequel.

There is half my creative writing side that focuses on crime novels. The other half of my creative writing side focuses on writing contemporary literary novels that deal with the human condition. These are two very different genres, but I find them both similarly satisfying in terms of creativity and storytelling.

One of the most profound lessons I have learned about writing over the past decade is that it takes a lot of time to master the craft. Many successful writers have made it later in life because of the demands writing takes on their energy and free time, particularly creative writing, which is a time-consuming craft, no different to painting, sculpting or song writing. Whilst it looks deceptively simple, it's one of the hardest crafts to master.

The other lesson that I've learned is that good writing—even very good writing—doesn't always get published, and that sometimes bad writing—even very bad writing—gets published. Writing is tied-in with publishing, and publishing is a business, and a business needs to make a profit.

Of course, that is not to say that commercially published books are not worthy of any literary merits or their authors talent-less—history has shown us that some of the best books ever published have been released by commercial publishers, which are profit-driven. *On The Road, In Search of Lost Time, Ulysses, War and Peace, One Hundred Years of Solitude, The Catcher In The Rye,* and countless other books by more recent authors, *White Teeth, The Book Thief, The Road, The Kite Runner, The Human Strain,* and some popular works by John Grisham, Stephen King, Patricia Cornwell and so on (and don't start arguing that genre writers and popular writers can't be good writers—nonsense. Good writing is good writing, period). Need I say more?

The dream of would-be novelists is to get a six- or seven-figure advance on their first novels. This rarely happens, but it does happen—but so does winning the lottery since people win every single week. If this is your intention, by all means, take that road, be ready for an up-hill battle, frustration and a lot of rejections. This does not mean you will not make it—I am a strong believer that at the end of the day you get what you want in life if you put the time and effort into it. There are no guarantees, of course, but persistence in learning the craft and sending the work out there has a lot to do with those big advances and successes some of 'those' writers have had.

In the past five years, the publishing world has changed dramatically as a result of technology and provides authors the possibility to self-publish at virtually no cost, or set-up their own independent publishing outfit. For writers new to the game, this can be both liberating and a curse.

Whether you decide to go the traditional way, self-publish, or set-up an independent press, the rules of the game are the same—unless you are dedicated to the craft of writing and make it the focus of your life, you will struggle and your work will suffer.

I have taught creative and professional writing for a few years now, and during that time I have had the pleasure to work with hundreds of students. For every class of fifteen or so students, only one or two on average had what it took. Sometimes none. The idea of being an author appealed to them more than the writing and storytelling—a dangerous way of thinking, particularly at the beginning of one's writing career.

In this book, I hope to share with the would-be-novelist or new novelist what I have learned, and what I believe would be of use to your craft and career. Of course those involved in other aspects of creative writing might also find some of this advice useful, even if just as a source to pass on to their own writing students.

This is not a 'how-to' book on how to master the craft—there are too many good books on that subject already. It's a book that will discuss what it is to be a writer, how you fit into the writing world, and how to approach the craft level-headed and realistically, with some *tips* on the various techniques of fiction. If you're looking for an in-depth instruction manual on writing fiction, this is not the book for you. Choosing writing as a career is not for the faint-hardhearted. As a would-be novelist, you are alienating yourself from society, common people, common jobs, common careers. You are putting the fear of your future in your parents, your family, your spouse and everyone around you. This can be regarded as extremely brave by some and extremely silly by others.

You are a dreamer, and the world doesn't need another dreamer. Why don't you just get a regular job and write on the side?

Think of *A Guide For The New Novelist* as psychotherapy for the new novelist. I am going to take you by the hand and tell you everything *I know* about being a novelist. It's not the bible, and it's not essential reading for everyone, but if I can save you some time and trouble, then I will have achieved what I have set out to do.

Enjoy the journey.

Laurent Boulanger

THE QUALITY OF YOUR WORK

"Write. Rewrite. When not writing or rewriting, read. I know of no shortcuts."

—Larry L. King,

Creative writers are sensitive people otherwise they wouldn't be able to draw on their emotions to write. That being said, those who do not write or have no creative outlet are also sensitive people (one would hope), but they do not offer their minds to the world to dissect, hence they do not suffer the fear of writing and seeing their work being analyzed. Arguably, other creative people suffer from the same agony since their work is on display for the whole world to criticize and judge.

As writers, we are paranoid and defensive by nature. We fear that we are not up to it, that what we have written is not worthy of being published, that other writers are better than us, that past masters of the craft are geniuses, and we are doomed from the start. In spite of this we persist with writing because there is nothing else we would rather do. Writing has chosen us, and not the other way around. We write because it makes sense of life and gives us a purpose beyond waking up in the morning, going to work and coming back home. It offers us the opportunity to be individuals in a world where everyone is more often than not treated like a number. But for me, it's also therapeutic. It helps me to understand myself and others better. By looking at the lives of those who are not me, by exploring what it would be like to be faced with situations I haven't had to face, I sympathize with people who are not my age, my gender or from my culture.

Writing can also cure boredom. There are many hours in the day, and even for those of us who have a day job, a lot of time is leftover to do as we please. Boredom is a killer, and writing is a boredom killer, unless you write something that bores you to death. When you choose writing as a vocation or a side occupation, you are less likely to be bored because you can always turn to writing, or reading if you've run out of energy for the day.

I'm not sure what you will get out of your writing, but if you are driven to be a writer in a non-egotistical way, you have more to gain than to lose. You need to accept that writing does not have to be about commercialization only, and that it's first and foremost a craft. Write for the love of writing, not because you believe it's going to be a good way to make easy money. It's not going to be an easy way to make money. Even successful writers will tell you that. Just like any other craft, you have to love the craft first, and then, if you are lucky and are in the right place at the right time with the right book, you might make money from your book, and maybe even good money, and in some cases, you might even become rich. But I don't recommend going with the goal of making because if you seriously want to make money, there are easier ways to make money then betting on getting a bestseller on the market. Go into banking or shares or real estate instead.

commercial publishing

The commercial publishing world has told us that if we do not get published, there is something wrong with our writing. And after decades of commercial publishing, we've come to believe this is like gospel. What we haven't been told is that publishing is commercial enterprise and that it's divided into two distinctive departments, namely acquisition and marketing. It's a two-headed monster. Your work might be great and is therefore selected for possible publication by an editor. It then gets past on to the marketing department, and if it is not convinced that enough copies will be sold, be damn about genius and good writing.

Or you might just get what you want, and the book is selected for publication and passes the 'marketing' test, in which case you're on your way, which is not necessarily a road paved with gold—you'll still have to deal with incompetent editors and spend a lot of time doing promotion for your book, which often means traveling away from your friends and family. Or you might get a good editor who will help you to make your book much better than it initially was by doing countless re-writes through back-and-forth correspondence.

For all the successes we read about, we never hear of the frustrations that mid-list and low-list writers experience. Some writers spend two years writing a novel that sells only a couple of thousand copies, even though the book has been published by a commercial publisher. As a result, the writer gets 'dumped' and it's virtually impossible to get another book published. One way around this is to write under a new name and begin the game all over again. It's actually easier for a new novelist to get published than one with a poor sales track record.

If you are going to play the writing-publishing game, be ready for disappointment, or don't even start. If disappointment doesn't scare you, and if you don't have huge expectations, and are ready to accept whatever may come, then you're more likely to persist and make some headway with your writing.

persistence

Persistence is the name of the game here, the same as with any other craft. The longer you stick to something, the more you practice, the better you'll get at it, the more likely someone is going to notice—but again, there is no guarantee in that either because life doesn't come with a guarantee. The only guarantee is that if you keep on writing on a regular basis *and* you improve on the craft by mastering fiction techniques, you *will* become a better writer.

Recently I had a student who told the rest of the class that an acceptance or a rejection letter from commercial publishing houses was a clear indication of the quality of her work. I told her that an acceptance or a rejection from a traditional publisher is not necessarily a reflection of the other (and some of my fiction has been published by commercial publishers in book form, and it's not my best work). I told her the story of James Lee Burke's novel *The Lost Get-Back Boogie,* which had been nominated for a Pulitzer Prize after being rejected by one-hundred-and-eleven publishers for a period of nine years. Does this mean that his manuscript was of a lesser quality for the first eight years, and then suddenly of better quality in the ninth year, even though he hadn't changed a word in the story? Thanks to the persistence of his relentless agent, the novel ended being published by Louisiana University Press. At some stage Burke couldn't get anything published for years (and a huge gap of fourteen years before published hardcover novels), even though he had published before.

A rejection of your work is not a clear indication that the work is not worthy of publication. This is what some publishers want writers to believe so that they keep a stronghold on the industry and decide what should be published and not published (and of course this has now changed with e-book publishing and print-on-demand publishing).

In all common sense, the best judge of your writing is *you*. Not your spouse, your children, your grand-parents, your neighbors, the local librarian or the junior publisher at a big publishing house. If you are uncertain about the quality of your writing, it is most likely because you do not read enough.

Reading a lot provides you with the skills to be able to evaluate your writing against those who have mastered the craft, and if you cannot do that, you are not ready to send your work into the market. You must keep reading and writing until you are able to figure out where the quality of your writing stands.

reading and writing

Stephen King in his book *On Writing* advises that those who want to write need to read—a lot. If you are not reading at least one novel a week, you will not learn, or the learning curve will be long and tedious. He states like many other seasoned novelists:

"If you want to be a writer, you must do two things above all others: read a lot and write a lot. There's no way around these two things that I'm aware of, no shortcut."

I hear a lot of writers who say, "Yes, yes, this is old school, we'll all know that." And yet, they don't bother reading, which might explain why the mantra is repeated over and over— *write, write, writer, read, read, read.*

faith and arrogance

It's all fine, of course, to have faith in your ability to judge the quality of your own work. However, the other side of the coin is that too many writers believe themselves to be geniuses, the voice of their generation. As a result, they do not improve the craft, and they dismiss advice from anyone.

Here's a great one from one of my students:

"I don't need to learn grammar. That's my style. Grammar is censorship, and it ruins my style."

Can you see how ridiculous this sounds? It's like a surgeon who says, "I don't need to know where the organs are. I'll just cut and see what happens—that's my style."

You can't learn to write without learning the fundamentals of writing—grammar and technique—the same as you cannot learn how to operate on patients without knowing where the organs are in the body.

Whilst I do believe that you are the best judge of your own writing, as a writer, your ego is also your worst enemy. Your ego can fool you into believing that everything you write—even your shopping list—is a stroke of genius, and that the world will eventually see you for what you are. If you are ego-driven, the focus will be on you, the writer, and not on the writing and the storytelling. This is dangerous and counter-productive. Ego-driven writers refuse to learn the craft, refuse to edit, refuse to take on-board some well-meaning advice from seasoned professionals.

critical appraisal

Is there anyone you can turn to assess your writing when you are at a total loss? Of course, there is, but it's not easy to find those people, mainly because they are too busy writing—they are professional writers.

Another group of people are literary or talent agents. They are hard to approach and are very busy, but if your work is very good, they will let you know and might even decide to represent you. If an agent represents you, it says something about your work to a degree. A good agent will not charge you anything for representation. It's all part of running the business. Stay away from agents who charge. They are some genuine agents who charge upfront for expenses, but there are also many sharks at sea, so it's best to avoid agents who charge altogether.

There are also manuscript assessment services out there, but once again watch out for sharks. Since the popularity of self-publishing, many callous individuals and companies take advantage of naive writers, and often manuscripts are assessed by people who have less experience than you have (I could name a company or two, but the defamation lawsuits would start arriving within a couple of days). I recommend talking to other writers and finding out through word-of-mouth who they would recommend to assess or provide you with feedback on your work.

You can join a writers group, but depending on the level of experience from those in the group, it might be counter-productive. A really harsh and unfair criticism by someone ignorant might sabotage your inspiration and love of writing forever. Join a group if you must, but be careful who is in the group, and if you feel unmotivated at the end of a few sessions, you're better off spending more time writing or reading. There is no point in being in a writing group if it's going to soul-destroying.

the writer as apprentice

So where exactly do you stand in terms of the quality of your work if you find that it's not up to scratch? If you are new to the game, you're an apprentice, and you should spend the next five to ten years learning the craft—that is writing every day and reading every day. You are allowed to make mistakes. You *must* make mis-takes, otherwise you are not learning. You must fear the writing; you must fear failure; and you must fear that nothing might ever come out of this. This is a common state of mind for all creative people. We are human, and we live with self-doubt all the time. If you find that hard to believe, have a one-on-one conversation with artists whom you come across, and you'll see how fear grips every single one of them.

Ann Brashares, writer of the bestsellers *The Sisterhood of the Traveling Pants* series gives solid advice: "For me, starting is really hard so I really need to give myself permission to do a bad job. I always give myself time to write total nonsense for as long as I need to release the pressure...there are moments of deep, deep doubts, and you have to have faith that your initial idea was good and just muddle through."

And if this scares you before you even begin your career, you have no business in trying to become a novelist. There are other pursuits in life that don't plague you with self-doubt every time you choose to participate in them.

GRAMMAR

"A man's grammar, like Caesar's wife, should not only be pure, but above suspicion of impurity."

— Edgar Allan Poe

Grammar and fiction techniques are to the novelist what a hammer and nails are to the carpenter. These are your tools, and you must learn to master them if you want to become proficient at your craft. If you don't like grammar, you don't like language, your don't like words, and, honestly, how could you possibly like writing?

The lazy writer does not learn grammar and does not want to learn grammar. It takes time, it's hard, it's annoying, she complains.

It's not true.

Grammar is fascinating.

Last month I ran a workshop in creative writing at my local community centre on request from the course coordinator. I touched on grammar, and as a result, every student wanted me to run a grammar workshop in the future.

If you are a serious writer, do not believe that grammar is the enemy—it's your friend. Learning grammar will make you a better writer, and who doesn't want to become a better writer?

When I studied creative writing at junior college, my

grammar teacher had a military-style approach to his teaching. He demanded that we do the work every single week. For me, it wasn't difficult because I was totally fascinated by writing and language, and hence the learning of grammar become addictive and an eye-opener.

As we have seen in the previous chapter, making grammatical errors out of ignorance is not style—it's laziness. Making grammatical errors purposely when you know the rules is *style*. Writers do this for effect. This is even more true with fiction than with non-fiction.

And you shall not begin a sentence with a coordinating conjunction.

Because it doesn't work.

Of course it does.

See what I mean?

Sometimes breaking the rules works, but you cannot break the rules unless you know what the rules are. Run-in sentences are okay with fiction because they form part of a style. Some writers—the late Morris Lurie for example—made a career of writing grammatically incorrect fiction. But it was obvious this was done as a stylistic device and not because of ignorance. Young writers often confuse this with a deviance of refusing to follow standards and choose to not learn grammar as a result.

You don't need to buy a book on grammar the size of the bible to get going. The best books tend to be those written for primary or secondary school students, those that are exercise books in nature. They show you the rules, explain them, and then you get to practice and check the answer. More often than not, they are basic in nature, but that's all you need.

Here's a quiz. Define:

- nouns
- pronouns

- verbs
- adverbs
- adjectives
- conjunctions
- prepositions
- interjections
- phrases
- clauses
- gerunds
- present participle
- past participle

What is a gerund phrase? Did you know that it can function as subject or object in a sentence? Did you know that in the great majority of cases a word in a sentence is defined by its function rather that its meaning? *Love* is a word that can function as a noun, verb and adjective, but this function can only be defined when you see it in a sentence. By changing its spelling, it can also function as a gerund and be used in clauses and phrases that function as subjects and objects. If you don't understand what I am talking about, you need to brush up on your grammar.

punctuation

Here's a common myth from those who are grammatically illiterate: just place a comma when you take a breath. Wrong. If you're an asthmatic (and I was one for twenty years, so I know what I'm talking about), you'd place a comma after every single word. The place of a comma in a sentence is regulated by specific grammatical rules, which, if you are not familiar with, you cannot use to your advantage.

an editor will fix it

Here's another myth: I don't need to know grammar; an editor will fix it.

No, an editor will not fix it. Firstly, a manuscript filled with grammatical errors is off-putting. It's a sign of an amateur. Publishers are not in the habit of buying novels filled with grammatical errors, particularly from new novelists. One of the best ways to stand from the crowd is to ensure that your work is as grammatical error-free as possible. And the best way to achieve this is to learn your grammar.

No short cuts.

Learn your grammar.

Grammar and self-publishing

If you decide to go the self-publishing path, this is even more important. If you do not use an editor, there is nothing between you and readers. The work you write is the work readers will read—with all the grammatical errors included. Readers do not have an auto, real-time grammar correction device attached to their brains to filter grammatical errors in your book. You will come across as unprofessional and unreliable.

grammar and editing

I think it would be hard to argue here that if you don't know your grammar, you cannot edit your work effectively. This goes without saying. A solid grounding of grammar will provide you with the ability to become a better editor of your own work—or another person's work for that matter—so don't believe that you will be a good writer in the long run if you don't bother learning your grammar. It's not going to happen.

Be aware that it's much easier to understand the rules of grammar than to implement them. Just like mastering the craft of fiction, it takes time to implement your newly-found grammatical knowledge into your work. If you decide to go ahead and purchase a grammar workbook (which I recommend you do), then go over it 2-3 times. The first time might be a bit of struggle; the second time will be easier; and the third time, you'll know as much as you need to know.

Keep a grammar reference book on your desk (I recommend *21st Century Grammar Handbook* because it's designed like a dictionary, and you can go straight to the problem at hand*)*, and when you are editing your own work, always check whatever it is that you're uncertain about. Don't be lazy about this. This is how you learn, and how you will get better at grammar.

Want to become a better writer?

Learn your grammar.

FICTION TECHNIQUE

"It's none of their business that you have to learn to write. Let them think you were born that way."

—Ernest Hemingway

Fiction technique is not grammar. Fiction techniques are unspoken rules on how to make your fiction more effective. Good editors know fiction techniques, even if they don't write themselves, and can sharpen a manuscript. However, it is best for a writer to master those techniques because it will not only give a good, first impression, but it will also save an editor a lot of work and headaches.

You can learn a lot of fiction techniques by reading fiction, and then by re-reading the same book and analyzing the narrative.

There are also good books on mastering the various fiction techniques. Writer's Digest has a vast collection, some better than others, but you can still learn a lot even from the ones that are average. There are other books on techniques published by other publishers, so check what's available online and what other readers think of those books. And of course, there is also the Writer's Digest Magazine that covers a lot of ground, but it's not specifically aimed at fiction writers, but at writers from all walks of life, in-cluding scriptwriters, poets, non-fiction writers, blog writers and so on.

Here's a list of what you need to learn in order to become an accomplished novelist:

- openings
- characterization
- sensory details and descriptions
- dialogue
- settings
- endings
- narrator's point of view
- paragraphing
- story arc
- re-writing and editing

There are many other aspects of fiction writing that you will come across, but they all fall under one of those sections. It is not the purpose of this book to provide you with in-depth instructions on all the fiction writing techniques—its purpose is to guide you so that you are confident in terms of knowing what's ahead of you and plan a practical way to learn the craft. There are many good books on the craft of fiction that cover the different techniques.

I will touch on some of the techniques but just as a guide rather than an in-depth analysis. You cannot learn one skill without learning the other. It's a process of learning everything at once, a little bit on a daily basis. Implement what you have learned into your writing. Once you have learned a new skill, go back to what you have written the previous day, and see if you can improve on it. Think of the process as learning how to drive a car. You have to know how to steer the car, how to brake, how to indicate, how to accelerate and so on. A single skill is not going to make you a driver, and mastering one only is certainly not going to get your there either. It's the same with writing. You have to learn everything a little bit at a time, and practice all that you have learned on a daily basis. If you don't practice (just like learning how to drive), you will not improve. You wouldn't expect a guitar player to become better at playing without practice, so why would a writer be the exception?

Stephen King simplifies the whole process in his book *On Writing* by stating:

"In my view, stories and novels consist of three parts: narration... description, and dialo-gue."

All the techniques fit into those three re-quirements somehow.

OPENINGS

"Books are the treasured wealth of the world and the fit inheritance of generations and nations."

—Henry David Thoreau

When readers grab a book from a shelf at a bookshop to look at it, they read the opening first. The entire book is judged by its opening more than anything else in the book. This is also true of e-book versions of novels, which can be sampled. Amazon, for example, lets readers sample the first few pages of Kindle electronic books in order to decide on a purchase, which means buyers determine more often-than-not (particularly with books whose authors they are unfamiliar with) to purchase a book based on the opening sentence, paragraph or page. If it doesn't meet their expectations, they simply won't buy the book.

the art of openings
Choose ten novels. Read the openings. Select the one that would work well with your story. If you haven't found an opening that appeals to you, get more novels, preferably in the genre you are writing in, and you'll find something eventually that will grab your attention and imagination.

There are fiction techniques for the opening scene of a novel. You can start with describing a setting. You can start with a social commentary. You can start with dialogue. You can start with a starling revelation.

Here is an example of the opening scene of my literary novel *Addiction*:

> Today is the day Danielle is going to find out her sister is a complete bitch.
> Danielle arrives at the front of her apartment after a long day at work—eight hours in the confinement of an over-air conditioned office where everything is grey and windowless. She lives next door to a private hotel that accommodates junkies, drunks and other patrons who are incapable of finding what others would consider *normal* accommodation. In the middle of the night, she sometimes hear someone scream, objects and furniture thrown around, cop cars and ambulances blaring their sirens, but she ignores all of it. There's been ten deaths in the hotel in the past ten years, but they all took place on the inside between the patrons. A drunk says something, a junkie gets offended, and before you know it, they are at each other's throat with meat cleavers and kitchen knives.

In this sample, I have started with foreshadowing—I have told readers what is going to happen in the hope that they will want to read on to learn how exactly Danielle going to find out that her sister is a bitch. Then, I set the scene so that we get a solid and realistic picture of the environment she is in.

Here's another example from one of my crime novels, *First Kill*:

> The call came at 2.15 a.m. on Thursday the 20th of February.
> No one ever called me in the middle of the night, unless it was murder.
> The hottest February for over a hundred years had swept over the city. I remember the day clearly, not only because of the middle-of-the-night telephone call, but also because of the *Herald-Sun*'s headline 'Sizzler of the Century', which would be splattered over its a.m. edition in a few hours.

Here I've begun with an action, a date and a time, which

helps with the suspension of disbelief. When readers have a day and time, it feels 'more real'. This is followed by the reason for the call, which is 'murder', a hook to make readers want to read on. And then I describe the setting of the protagonist.

Another novel in the same series, *Second Cut*, begins this way:

> The frail body of a young girl lay in a pool of mud alongside Albert Park Lake, next to one of the few remaining elm trees.

The book opens straight with a crime-scene, which is also a good way to hook the readers.

Or you can start with dialogue, as in *Third Victim*, the third book in the series:

> 'She was found thrown over a high-steel fence, in the back courtyard of a group of flats, her armpit impaled on a spike,' explained Senior Sergeant Frank Moore when I questioned him about the location of the victim.

There are endless ways to open a novel, and you need to choose one that's the most appropriate to your story and your genre. With crime books, a good hook at the start usually gets the ball rolling. With literary novels, you have a little more time to set the scene, but it doesn't mean that you can't start with a hook—a sentence or a paragraph that *hooks* the reader into the story. Keep in mind that when someone wants to buy a book, she normally opens the first page or so to see if the story is what is expected. As previously mentioned, even with e-books, readers read the first few pages in order to judge if the writing is in par with what they expect. After all, it's very risky to buy a book if you have no idea of what the story and style is like. This is of course less of a risk if the writer is well-known, and the writing is consistent from one novel to another. That's in fact how famous writers develop their reputations and have a fan base of their work.

the reader or the story?

Of course the question remains here whether you should worry about the reader or the story? Do you write an opening hook in the first paragraph of your novel because it serves the story best or just to hook readers? In most cases, you can do both. Sometimes the hook will seem artificial, so don't bother. You must first and foremost serve the story, make it the best you can, and sometimes starting with a hook is not the best way to do that.

One way to solve this dilemma is to write two opening paragraphs—one with a hook and one without a hook—and analyze which one works best for the story you are writing.

The opening of *Addiction* was originally written without the opening sentence and began with what is now the second paragraph.

Here are the two openings:

With hook:

Today is the day Danielle is going to find out her sister is a complete bitch.

Without hook:

Danielle arrives at the front of her apartment after a long day at work—eight hours in the confinement of an over-air conditioned office where everything is grey and windowless.

In this case, I felt that the opening with a hook was far more effective and dramatic. It grabs the reader straight way, and it foreshadows what's going to happen. It's also a good introduction to the whole novel because that's what the story is more-or-less about.

dialogue

There are also techniques for dialogue. In hard-boil crime fiction, short and sharp dialogue is preferred. In descriptive fiction, long dialogue is preferred. Look at the type of books you would like to write, and study the dialogue. How is it set? How much is being said? How much is not being said? How is the writer breaking the gram-matical rules to achieve the fiction techniques required in the story?

Think and analyze. Don't be lazy. That's why you must read fiction, read books on fiction techniques (there are hundreds of them on Amazon), and analyze techniques from other writers you admire. Imitate if you have to (not copy, which is not the same thing) until you master the techniques. Painters do it. Musicians do it. Writers have to do it to if they want to learn.

Basic fiction techniques

The basic essential techniques of fiction, irrespective of the genre, are narrative, sensory details and dialogue. This is not the same as storytelling. You can master the techniques and still come up with a bad story and poor characterization.

The narrative is what you see on the page, the way the sentences are structured, your voice. This usually occurs after a period of time and by writing a lot.

The sensory details are basically usage of your 'five senses' by describing settings, people or situations, namely smell, sound, taste, sight and touch. Some genres have more, some have less. But whatever you do, use one of them at least once in each new scene or chapter. It will ground your fiction in reality, and the readers will be more likely to believe in your story.

Good storytelling is the ability to make readers believe that your story is true. Well, they know it's not true like in real life, but they want to believe it's true. They are willing to believe it's true, which is why they have picked up your book. Your job is to use all the fiction techniques at your disposal to make this invented world as real as reality, even if it's set on Mars or in an imaginary world.

With details, always aim for precise details instead of vague details. Don't tell us it's a beautiful morning—this can be interpreted in different ways for readers depending on where they live in the world and what they consider to be beautiful. Instead, describe what a beautiful day looks like. The color of the sky, the smell and taste in the air, the temperature on the skin, the surrounding sounds. Use the five senses effectively when detailing your story.

Dialogue is best learned through practice and observation. Realistic dialogue is not real life conversation. All the boring bits are cut out. It's more dramatic than real life dialogue. In real life, we don't argue all the time, or we would go insane. In fiction dialogue needs to be dramatic, hence the characters have to argue. This not only causes conflict, but it is the essence of drama. Without conflict, you have no drama and no tension and nothing to push the story forward. Your readers will be bored and they will not finish the story.

Every time you have two characters come together, have them argue about something. They don't have to beat each other over the head about it, but just enough to get the dramatic tension going. Even two lovers in bed after they have finished making love can argue a little. A little tug-of-war pushes the story for-ward.

One effective way to learn how to write believable dialogue is to read screenplays. Screenplays have a lot of dialogue in them, and a good screenplay has solid dramatic dialogue. Using screenwriting dialogue techniques for fiction can be very effective at keeping the plot moving forward and keeping tight the dramatic tension in a scene.

Let's move on now. Make sure you spend time mastering grammar and the techniques of fiction—these tools will help you write dramatic stories readers will want to read.

And remember that if you want to write novels: *write, write, write, read, read, read.*

No short cuts.

SCHOOLS OF WRITING

"I had no contacts in the literary world, no sense of the process a book must go through, no ability to discuss the craft of literature, and on a day-to-day basis, no time to dedicate myself to it. At N.Y.U., I got those things."

—David Wingrave, *New York Times*

If you want to be a novelist, you do not need to study creative writing at college or university. Countless successful and less successful writers have written and published novels without attending a writing class. If you want to be a surgeon, you need to study because you cannot learn the skills in the confinement of your bedroom. If you want to become a lawyer, you need to study because you cannot be licensed to practice law without passing a bar exam. If you want to write a novel, you just need to sit at your desk and write a novel. There is no law or authority that grants you the rights to write a novel. It's up to you, and you can do it any time, on any day of the year.

Having said that, some would argue the merits of a college education in creative writing. It's true that it can be beneficial for *some*. I, myself, studied creative writing for years, but my reasons are different from yours.

The other issue is that it can keep you focused. If you are the type of writer who is easily distracted and cannot focus on the task at hand (in which case, I would argue it might be best you do not choose writing novels as a vocation), the study of creative writing at a college will help you to focus on the big picture. Beware, however, that college writing classes will not make you a novelist any more than sitting at home watching movies will make you a film director. There are no qualifications required to become a novelist. As long as you sit at your desk and write novels, you're a novelist.

Another advantage of attending college and studying creative writing is that you might be able to network with some people who might be able to help place your work with an agent or a publisher. In the great majority of cases, this is a myth and seldom happens for a couple of reasons. The first one is if you are studying creative writing at college, it means that you haven't mastered the craft yet, and the odds are your writing is not up to scratch. If, however, you do produce good writing, keep in mind that those who teach creative writing have as much trouble selling their work than you will one day.

Teachers who focus on teaching writing tend to be writers themselves, but the writing does not support them, and they need to make money on the side, otherwise they wouldn't survive.

Myth: Those who cannot do, teach.

The reality is that the great majority of novelists cannot make a living from writing novels alone, even the published ones, hence they have to derive their incomes from some other activity. Teaching writing is one way to stay in the industry.

If you have no intention of teaching creative writing, you shouldn't study creative writing at college. You will end up with a MFA in Creative Writing that will be of no use to you or anyone else. The only thing you can with an MFA in writing is teach writing, or get a job that is someone linked to writing, but is not writing itself—working for a publishing firm, working for a talent agency, or any job that requires some type of creative writing skills.

John Gardner in his book *Becoming A Novelist* states that doing an MFA in Writing will in fact make you a better writer and will offer you more opportunities to teach creative writing, although he also argues that there are far more MFA graduates than jobs available in the teaching of creative writing. He also states that the great majority of novelist cannot support themselves through writing, so teaching creative writing is one way to still be actively involved in the field.

I personally know very good writers who are commercially published and have won countless national and international awards over the years and still have to teach at university to make ends meet. John Coetzee, for example, is a winner of countless international prizes, including two Booker Prizes and a Nobel Prize in Literature, and yet he worked as a professor of literature at the University of Cape Town in South Africa, and later on retirement as a research fellow at the University of Adelaide in Australia. The fact that he earned a PhD in linguistics and his research was on the style of Samuel Beckett didn't hurt his writing or his ability to gain employment in creative writing when the writing itself was not providing enough income.

If you must go to college and have no attention of teaching creative writing in the future, study anything but creative writing. Become an expert at something you will be able to use with your creative writing. Think Patricia Cornwell and forensic science. John Grisham and law. Robin Cook and medicine. Michael Crichton and science. Learn a skill that you can implement in your writing, and this way you'll have some life experience and knowledge to draw from, otherwise you are going to end up writing novels about writers (whilst *On The Road* and countless other novels from that period are about writers, that's all in the past now, and nowadays very few novels about the writing life sell or get published).

If you don't want to become an expert at anything, then become an expert of the human condition because that's what novel writing involves. You have to be fascinated by people in a way that it will force you to study the human condition in your books. Even with genre writing, like with the works of Cornwell, Grisham, Cook and Crichton, the authors study the human condition but place their protagonists in a field of work or industry that fascinates readers—the police, law, medicine and science. Readers love to learn about industries and environments they are not necessarily familiar with, so it's a huge advantage for a novelist to have superior knowledge of a field or location and bring forth something unique to the storytelling form.

One other advantage of going to college, is that you are more likely to earn a higher salary when you graduate than without any qualifications. However, there is nowadays no guarantees at all. Too many schools operate like a racket as they promote their courses in glossy brochures and lovely, eye-catching websites, and will let just about anyone in if the economy is tough and faculty members want to keep their jobs. No students = no money. Let's be clear here that when an education institution is private and profit-driven, you cannot always be certain of what you are getting in terms of value. After all, you are paying for this, and the goal of the institution is to make a profit, not necessarily to provide you with the best education possible. Having said that, some institutions that are well-regarded have no problem attracting students, and those places spend more time and effort on delivery of quality courses. They tend to be very selective in whom they accept, and they can be very expensive.

A MFA in the US can set you back with a debt of around $50,000 or more. That's a huge debt to carry if you're not going to get any work out of what you have learned.

If money is not an issue, and you are from a family that can support any of your passions, by all means, don't let the cost factor stop you. But be aware that, once again, doing an MFA in Writing is not going to turn you into an instant novelist upon graduation. You will, however, meet other students who are as hungry as you are to learn everything they can about writing, and this can be a relief since novelists in society are not taken seriously unless they are successful.

When are you going to get a real job?

One of the downsides of studying creative writing at college is if you happen to be taught by someone who knows little about writing, but who just happens to be there by default, chance or whatever other life situations has made that person share a class with you and tell you what you supposedly need to know in order to become a novelist.

A while back a film starring Sean Connery and titled *Finding Forester* came out to little acclaim. The film is about writers—a reclusive, successful writer; a young ambitions writer; an angry unsuccessful writer; a faculty that teaches writing but dwells not much on the writing, but on academic prestige. I recommend you get yourself a copy and watch it. You will see the importance of sitting at one desk and writing, and how creative writing classes can in fact be counter-productive at times if you are taught by bad teachers. Some will abhor genre writing, and will not accept anything in any genre, other than literature. Run way. There is nothing wrong with literature, but you need to decide what you want to write, and not let someone else decide for you, otherwise you are going to end up bitter, like the antagonist in *Finding Forester*.

Now, some further counter-argument here is that some very good writers have in fact studied creative writing and do believe that it has helped them a lot. Melissa Bank, who wrote the bestselling novel *The Girl's Guide to Hunting and Fishing*, states that having done an M.F.A. in writing has taught her a lot about the craft in terms of technique. What she has learned has given her the skills to be able to edit her own work (something I will discuss later on in this book, and the importance of editing your own work). In her experience, editors no longer edit books, but basically try to get a deal for the book, and hence the bulk of the editing is really left to the author. James Lee Burke, nominated for a Pulitzer Prize, also studied creative writing. The Australian writer Garry Disher won a scholarship in the USA to study creative writing, and since then he has become one of the most prolific writers in his country, producing crime fiction, literary novels and children's books, all of which have won national awards (and he had to teach creative writing for a while to make ends meet even though he had several books in print and many literary awards under his belt).

There is the odd argument that writing cannot be taught, which is untrue. It's like saying painting and music cannot be taught. Writing is a craft, and fiction writing can be taught. As previously discussed, one of the best ways to learn is to read and write on a regular basis. If you are lucky to be enrolled in a MFA in Writing with good teachers, you will learn faster. Not all writing teachers are good teachers, hence if you do decide to go down the road of studying creative writing, make sure you are very selective in terms of where to study and who is teaching there. Sometimes you have teachers who have little output in terms of creative writing, but they are very good teachers and can analyze other writers' work with ease. At other times, you might have a very good writer on the faculty, but this person happens to be a terrible teacher with an attitude, which can be detrimental to a young writer who needs inspiration and encouragement.

If you study writing at college or university, you will inevitably have to take part in a writers' workshop. That is a place where all the writing students are going to read your writing and offer their opinions. Some people can be quite nasty, and if you don't have a solid backbone, it can shatter your confidence.

In the film *Wonder Boys,* adapted from the novel of the same name by Michael Chabon, there is a scene set at university where students are taking part in a workshop. One of the female students tears apart the work of a young male writer when in fact his writing is brilliant. Without the intervention of a good teacher, this could have been the end of the writer's career. The young writer, as it turns out, ends up with a publishing contract before the end of the film. Chabon, as a writer, has clearly used a lot of his own experience when writing the novel, and whilst the film is very dramatized for the sake of serving the story line and the medium of cinema, there are some good truths in there for those who want to know what it's like to be a young, novice novelist and an old novelist with a writer's block who is forced to teach to make ends meet.

In conclusion here, if you do choose to go down the track of studying creative writing at college or university, make sure it's a positive experience that provides you with the energy and stamina required to persist with the learning of the craft. In the words of John Gardner:

"If you feel miserable in your writers' workshop, you should talk about your misery in private with the teacher, and if things don't improve, you should quit. A bad writing class doesn't only fail to teach writing, it can make one give up."

There—I couldn't have said it better myself.

THE WORKSPACE

"I have pictures of family members all around my workspace and I like to keep a lot of them right at eye level. Memories are significant and are often the basis of entire novels of mine."

—Warren Adler

Writing is time-consuming. Even if you write fast, you are still going to have to spend hours and days at a desk in order to produce something long enough to be called a novel. To do this, you'll need a place where you can sit by yourself with minimum distractions, and prefe-rably at a specific time of the day and no less than five days a week, just like a regular job.

There are—and I am acutely aware of this, so whatever I tell you is advice, not gospel—writers out there who prefer to work in cafes, libraries, public parks and so on. They find the confinement of one place too boring and difficult to work from.

Margaret Atwood does not have a writing space she uses when working on her novels. She writes on airplanes, airports, hotel rooms and so on. She does have a couple of writing desks, but she never uses them and prefers to write on the floor. It works for her, and that's all that matters.

I prefer to work at a desk with a view, nothing overly distracting, but nothing so boring that you feel that you're in a prison cell. Ideally, a view of the ocean, the beach or a park is what works best for me. Try to set up your desk underneath a window so that you get a lot of natural light. Unless you're a zombie, daylight is not going to hurt you.

Buy yourself a comfortable chair. After all, you are going to spend more time on that chair than anywhere else, other than your bed (and on some days, more time than in your bed), so it makes sense to buy a comfortable chair. You don't need to spend a fortune on a good chair—there are plenty of comfortable second-hand chairs out there. One with wheels attached is always good because it makes it easy to stroll from one side of the room to the other when you need to grab one of your novels or reference books in order to check a detail whilst working on your manuscript.

Get a desk big enough for your tools, reference books, and whatever you fancy that keeps you going.

Place photos or book jacket covers of you favorite authors on the walls of your study if that inspires you.

Do not have a television in your writing room, or anything that's going to distract you from doing the writing itself. If you are addicted to the Internet and find it a distraction, do not have the Internet connected to your computer when you are writing. You might need to have it on during the re-writing and research stage of the novel, but during the first draft, all you want to do is sit at that desk and keep writing, not be distracted by online news and the latest YouTube video.

Your writing space is your own personal sanctuary of creativity, your cocoon of ideas where no-one judges you and tells you what to do. Everything you write in this room should be free from other people's interruption, so make sure the door locked. Making it very clear to everyone who is living with you that when you are working in your writing room, no one has the right to disturb you, unless the house is on fire or someone is about to die. Running out of milk or having no hot water is not an emergency (unless you're the writer, of course!).

Another good idea is to place a 'do not disturb' sign on the door, and to instruct everyone in your household to obey it.

Some writers prefer to write in the basement, or a place that's not to pleasant because, for some reason, it provides them with discipline. It a little like those who prefer to workout in a gym fitted with old equipment rather the newest, latest, shiny machines. Old equipment tends to be associated with serious workouts rather than just look-at-me technology. Remember in the original *Rocky* movie, Balboa prefers to train outdoors and practices his fighting technique in a cold room hitting on beef carcasses. It does not mean you have to type in a cold room (or hit on beef carcasses), but a room that has character and isn't sterile can be much more inspiring. When Stallone wrote the *Rocky* screenplay, he did that in a studio apartment so small, he could close the door with his foot whilst lying in bed. He admitted that the lack of comfort forced him to sit at his desk and write. There was nothing else to do, and back in those days, no Internet to distract him.

The lesson here is that a room not filled with all the comforts of your lounge room can be beneficial if you really want to focus on the writing.

I personally know writers who write in cafes and bars because they are able to focus better on the work when there is noise around them. Some like the booze, some the coffee, some chatting to the waiters or waitresses. They share stories, and this can generate ideas of scenes in a novel. It takes a great deal of concentration to work with noise, and for those writers, this seems to work. They are forced to shut out the noise around them and really put everything into the story. If are bored sitting at home typing, then you might want to try this technique. Make sure you bring enough money for coffee, or the owner is going to be forced to charge you rent!

Music can also be a good motivator, particularly if you can find music that fits with the genre and pace of the story you are writing. If you are writing a fast-paced thriller, a thriller movie soundtrack can work well with the pace of your story. If you set your stories in the 1950s, for example, then some Miles Davis jazz from that era would put you in the right mood. Music is used in film to great effect, and it can work for you when working on your novel. Do not, however, play soundtracks filled with vocal songs. The lyrics can be quite distracting when you're trying to get your thoughts on paper, particularly if they are from a song you like. You'll be singing along the lyrics instead of focusing on your story.

Stephen King, oddly, likes to write with heavy rock or metal music in the background. This works for him, so at the end of the day, you need to find what works for you, what makes you more productive and what tools provide you with the desire to get more words on those pages. The right environment can make a whole world of difference in wanting or not wanting to write.

Another trick I have found is to regularly change rooms when working. It's a good idea to do the initial writing in one room, and the editing in another room. This makes it much easier to switch from the 'creative' mind to the 'editing' mind. The creative process is made up of those two parts, and having two working rooms can set your mind right. I would choose a messier room for the initial draft, and a more clinical room for the editing. The editing stage is a little like a medical procedure, where you have to cut out all those unnecessary words, replace others, add precise details, pace-out those paragraphs, sharpen the dialogue and make sure that the narrator's voice is constant throughout the story.

If you have a house with a garden, I suggest doing some of your writing outside. The natural light is good for you, and you won't feel as if you are constantly trapped between walls. Garden smells can also be quite pleasant, and it's known these can elevate your mood. Make sure that you have a comfortable chair for outdoor work because you will be sitting there for a few hours.

A local library can also be good if it's not too noisy. I wrote my first novel, which shall remained unpublished, by going every day to my local library and spending two hours writing the first draft long-hand. Then I want home and typed the hand-written text into my computer, which provided me with a chance to edit and progress to the second draft.

Libraries are also good because they provide you with access to a lot of references, particularly other authors' novels. There is no doubt that the Internet is a fantastic source of research, but to have thousands of novels at your fingertips is very useful. You can study how other authors begin their stories, introduce characters, write dialogue, provide sensory details and so on. If you're new to novel writing, it is very important to look at how successful writers have gone about doing the work. You can learn more from studying fiction than from attending writing classes.

A library also provides a right mood for those who need to focus on the work. After all, libraries are for reading and studying, so by working in such an environment, the tone will be set for you to pull up your sleeves and get the work done. The heating and cooling is also free, so this might be a huge advantage if you live in a part of the world where the weather is extreme on both sides of the scale.

In winter, make sure you have adequate heating in your writing room. If you're freezing in there, you are not going to want to spend much time working. The same thing applies to air conditioning in summer. It's impossible to work in a room that feels like the inside of an oven.

Finally, setting up a room where you do your writing on a regular basis forces you to take 'the writing' seriously. This is not much of a problem for those who find it easy to focus on writing as a career, but new novelists often wonder if they are not wasting time. A room dedicated for your writing will make that wishful-thinking goal of writing novels a serious vocation.

One on my favorite rooms to work in is the kitchen. It's

bright, the coffee machine is within reach, and it's spacious. I am not a big fan of being cramped in a small room to do my writing. I tend to feel claustrophobic in such an environment, and this stops me from wanting to go back the next day and do more work.

Whatever place you choose to work in, make it your own. It's all about productivity, and you need to find that special place, whether it be at home, at a cafe, at a public library, in a garden or the kitchen—a place where you produce the most amount of writing in the shortest amount of time. If you are like me and love writing, but you also have a life to live and other obligations to attend to, then when you sit down to write, you want to make sure you're not distracted by outside elements in order to get the writing done quickly and efficiently.

TIME MANAGEMENT

"Time is the most valuable coin in your life. You and you alone will determine how that coin will be spent. Be careful that you do not let other people spend it for you."

—Carl Sandburg

Set a writing schedule when you are going to be sitting at that desk and do some serious writing. Your room is ready with all the comforts you feel will help you to get the writing done. But the writing doesn't get done by itself. You still have to spend hours on end in front of a computer (or a typewriter, but not many writers write this way anymore for obvious reasons). Some writers work by the hour, others by the word. Stephen King writes two thousand words a day, in the morning, seven days a week, no matter what. Once he reaches the magic two-thousand words, he stops. John Grisham used to write before going to work between 5 a.m. and 7 a.m. when working on his first novel *A Time To Kill.* Lee Child works in the afternoons, six days a week for 80-90 days, and then takes the rest of the year off (most likely to promote the work rather than sit at the beach drinking Pina Colada all day). The point is, no matter what your method, you need to find what works for you and stick to it.

If you haven't written enough yet, and do not know what the best time of the day for writing is, then try different times until you figure out when you are the most productive. For me, it's mornings. First thing when I am up, I make myself a coffee, go to my desk and type. The writing comes easily. By the afternoon, I am tired and can't be bothered. The advantage of working in the morning is that by lunchtime the work is done for the day, and you won't feel guilty that you have not produced any writing. It also reduces the anxiety of having to write since you have already written for the day.

Others are busy all day with work or raising children, so they find the only writing time they have is when everyone else has gone to bed. I'm not sure how exactly they manage to do this because by the time night time comes, all I want to do is go to sleep, but these nocturnal writers make it work—everyone has a different clock when it comes to creativity and work, and you need to figure out if you're a morning, an afternoon or a night writer.

Another technique in terms of being productive that's quite effective is to write in short periods and have rests, but during those short periods, do nothing but write. I work best when I write for 45 minutes non-stop in full concentration, and then take a 15-minute break. During the 15-minute break, I try to do something physical, like sweeping the floor or working in the garden. When the 15 minutes are over, I'm ready to get back into the writing. I find that with short bursts of writing, I can write much more productively than if I sit at a desk and tell myself I have forever to fill up those pages.

Do not set one day aside per week and tell yourself that it's your writing day. It's best to set a time aside every day, even if it's just one hour, and stick to it. Once you are set in a daily routine, it's fairly easy to keep going. If you break the routine, it's harder to get back into it.

You'll also find that if you don't write until you're sick of it, then you'll be left with wanting more at the end of the session. Burning out at the desk is not a good way to keep oneself motivated. Treat your writing as if someone is paying you by the hour (or the word, whatever works for you). After all, you turn up to work when you know you are going to get paid, so you need to develop the same attitude when it comes to your writing. We live in a society that thrives on money-making activities, and hence it's very easy to feel unmotivated when doing work that does not pay immediately in terms of dollars and cents. To work with nothing but passion and dedication as the only forms of motivation is not an easy task, and one way to keep the enthusiasm going is to be disciplined with your writing.

Bestselling author and Pulitzer Prize winner Michael Chabon advises on time management:

"Keep a regular schedule and write at the same time every day for the same amount of time. That's it. That is the total sum of my wisdom."

He writes at nighttime between 10 p.m. and 4 a.m., four days a week.

IDEAS

"When a reader falls in love with a book, it leaves its essence inside him, like radioactive fallout in an arable field, and after that there are certain crops that will no longer grow in him, while other, stranger, more fantastic growths may occasionally be produced."

—Salman Rushdie

Where do ideas come from? That's one of the most common question novice novelists ask those who make a living from writing fiction. It seems incredible that someone can make up tens of thousands of words and create a whole world from nothing but imagination.

The truth is novelists do not get *all* their ideas from their imaginations. They are inspired by events around them, news items, books they read, conversations they hear, subjects they want to explore. If you want to be a novelist, or if you are already one but are running out of ideas, you only have to look at the world around you. Ideas are everywhere. But are they worth expending into a novel-length narrative?

If you have no interest in the world and people, then you won't care about writing or fiction. Fiction is the study of the human condition, whether it be literary or genre fiction, it's always the story of a person or a group of people, hence you have to have a genuine interest in people, otherwise you are better of writing non-fiction if you absolutely feel the need to write books.

When I begin a new novel, I get inspired by a theme first. What's a theme? It's basically an idea that's fleshed out into a sentence or a few words, almost like a philosophical statement. For example, 'Love is complicated.' You can write a whole novel about stories of people where love is complicated.

With a novel, you have the luxury of working on several themes at once, but I don't recommend more than two or three main themes, otherwise, your story is going to be all over the place.

I tell novice writers that whatever it is that keeps them up at two o'clock in the morning might just be a subject worth exploring in a novel. If you something intrigues you that much that it keeps you awake in the middle of the night, and you don't have the answers, explore them through fiction.

Another way to get ideas is to base your fiction on true events. In the majority of my crime novels, the backbone of the story was inspired by a true crime event that took place. I read many true crime stories, and when I came across one that I found fascinating enough, I used it as the inspiration for my novel.

You do not need authorization to adapt a true story to a novel. Nobody owns the copy-right to a true event, although some people can claim rights to their life stories, but this is a very grey area since they are many unauthorized biographies published every year. With crime stories, if you decide to write crime novels, then you can pretty much use anything you want.

Michael Connelly, one of the world's best-selling crime writers, doesn't use real life crime stories to develop his stories. Instead, he is friends with a lot of police officers, and he spends time with them and listens to their stories. He believes police officers are natural storytellers because of the amazing experiences they have, and as a result they love to share stories with anyone who will listen.

If you have the ability to tap into a field where others are willing to freely share information with you, use it by all means. It hasn't hurt Connelly's career, and it won't hurt yours.

With literature, I begin with a theme and a character to serve that theme. The character is always challenged by something (which is the essence of all fiction, otherwise you wouldn't have any dramatic tension). That 'something' is what the theme is about.

Sometimes a news article can inspire you to write a story. What you need to ask yourself before you even begin is 'Is this idea big enough for a novel?'. Not all ideas are strong enough to maintain the narrative length that a novel requires. Some are best suited to short stories, some to stage plays, some to screenplays. You need to make sure that the story you have in mind fits the medium you have chosen.

But how do you know?

A story with a lot of inner thoughts will not make a good film because films work best with action and dialogue, not voice-overs (they are exceptions out there, but that's just what they are—*exceptions.*)

One way to test your idea is just to go ahead and write the first chapter. You'll know immediately if the story you have decided to work on is suitable for fiction.

I like writing beginnings. An intriguing begin-ning can get you motivated to write the whole novel. Think of your beginning as the opening of a film. Write a scene that makes readers want to read on immediately. It doesn't matter what genre you are writing in, the beginning is what readers look at when they check your book at the bookshop or online. If your book is on Kindle, for example, then the free sample offered is the first few pages. Readers make a decision on whether they are going to read a novel or not based on the first page. Is it interesting enough? Is the narrative in the style they enjoy? Is it well written? Does the narrator have a 'voice'?

Here's an exercise for you: look through your bookshelves

and read the first page of several of your favorite novels. How do they begin? Do those beginnings make you want to read on or not? Once you find a beginning you like, take the same approach and see if it works with your idea. If not, try a different beginning.

Beginnings by themselves can be a great inspiration and spring-board for the whole novel. Keep in mind that whatever you are writing is not written in stone, and just because you have a written a whole opening chapter of a novel, it does not mean that you have to write the whole novel if you are not happy with the result. Start a new beginning and see where it takes you.

Ideas can also occur during conversations with people. As a novelist, like I have previously mentioned, you need to be interested in the human condition, and in this case, it won't hurt you to socialize on a regular basis, otherwise your understanding of human nature will be second-hand, and you'll risk creating characters who end up looking like cardboard cutouts from television shows, movies and other novels. Talking to people will show you what others are interested in, and it might just spark an idea for your own novel.

Margaret Atwood uses an 'image' as the basis of a new work of fiction. She sees an image in her mind and it intrigues her enough to begin a story. Sometimes this image will be found later on in her story, but it is the seed that provides her with the spark to begin a story that she believes enough to bother turning into a full-length novel.

The well of ideas is endless, and it depends only on whether you have enough curiosity, motivation and inspiration to draw on those ideas and turn them into stories. There is a human element in every event out there.

But what about science-fiction and other genres? Human nature is the same around the world, so if you set your story on Mars, for example, you can still draw from the same source of human emotions in a different time and setting. In fact, this might even get you to explore ideas within the theme you have chosen that you might not have thought about if you had set your story in the present time.

You can adapt your idea to any genre and setting. You can adapt an idea to your favorite genre, to the type of novels you like to read.

On a final word, ideas do not have to be unique. A misleading myth is that to write a novel, your idea must be unique and original. This puts off a lot of new novelists because they cannot think of anything that has never been done before. There is no such thing as a unique idea. Everything has been done before. New ideas tend to be a blend of two older ideas. It is not the uniqueness of your idea that matters, but the *interpretation* of that idea. This means the way you are going to tackle a story is going to be completely different from your fellow writer, even if you use the same idea as the basis of your story. Your own experiences and view of the world means that the way you are going to express your idea in fiction is going to be different from anyone else, and that's what's unique about your idea. Once again, it's not the idea that needs to be unique, but the *interpretation* of an idea.

If you are a young writer, you are more likely to have the voice of a young writer in your work, and for obvious reasons it's best to choose ideas that matter to you and that are close to your own experiences. Your writing is less likely to come across as stilted and your voice non-genuine. Be true to yourself when you write, and you readers will see the truth in the story.

WRITING TO IMPRESS

"Perfectionism is the voice of the oppressor, the enemy of the people. It will keep you cramped and insane your whole life."

—Anne Lamott

The story is the most important element of your fiction. Not you, the writer. Not your writing. The story. A fiction writer is a storyteller. You must love telling stories if you want to become a novelist.

Those who love the idea of calling themselves writers more than doing the writing and telling stories are the most likely to fail. They do not have the passion, they do not care about storytelling, and they do not care about readers. Ego is the most dangerous aspect of the new novelist. There are several reasons for that. Firstly, when you focus on the ego, you will be overwhelmed by self-doubt. *Am I good enough? Am I talented enough? Am I just wasting time?* The bottom line is it doesn't matter.

If you never make it as a novelist, nobody will care. Nobody is going to miss the books you have never written. During the first five to ten years of writing fiction, you will make mistakes, and you will produce some bad writing, and you should. If you don't make mistakes, you cannot learn. A painter learns by painting. A musician learns by hitting the wrong notes. A writer learns from her mistakes. You cannot learn how to master the craft of writing by constantly thinking about your self-worth as as a writer. It's self-defeating and robs you of the creative energy you need to keep on writing.

You *are not* your writing. Writing is something you do. Once you accept this, then you can concentrate on the writing itself and not on whether you have the talent to make it as a writer or not. Talent has little to do with it. Writing is not a natural skill we have acquired at birth. It's artificial, and it needs practice to be mastered. It's a craft. You should come to your writing with passion and desire because of the love of writing, not because you think the world is going to think highly of you by calling yourself a writer. The world doesn't care. Everyone is too busy living their lives, working out what to do with it, to be overly concerned about your place on this planet.

If you approach writing with true passion, you should never have to worry about whether you have what it takes to write good fiction or not. If you write and read every day, you will get better at it. It's common sense, it's logical and there is no doubt about it. As long as you are willing to learn from your mistakes and improve your craft, you will become a better writer, and the better you become at your craft, the more likely your work will be read by others.

Do not write to impress. Readers don't care how well you can craft a sentence. They care about storytelling. If you have a lavish style, and it's comes naturally, then by all means, use it. *White Oleander* by Janet Fitch, for example, is filled with sensory details and heavy prose, but it works. Why? Because Fitch doesn't force the writing—it's her style, a style she has developed after many years of writing. Hemingway is the master of stripped-down prose, and yet his work got published. Why? Because publishers and readers care more about storytelling than you showing off your writing skills.

Bestselling author Tom Clancy says, "Do not try to commit art. Just tell the damned story. It it is entertaining, people will read it, and the objective of writing is to be read...fundamentally writing a novel is telling a story."

Focus on the storytelling, and choose a style and a voice that make the story the best it can be. Do not write with the idea others will proclaim what a wonderful writer you are. It's self-defeating and serves no purpose. Write for the love of writing and leave the ego aside.

PLOTTING

"I hate when people ask what a book is about. People who read for plot, people who suck out the story like the cream filling in an Oreo, should stick to comic strips and soap operas. . . . Every book worth a damn is about emotions and love and death and pain. It's about words. It's about a man dealing with life. Okay?"

—J.R. Moehringer

There are two schools of writing out there—one believes in plotting a story, and the other believes plotting is pointless and forces a story to be predictable and contrived.

Here's what I believe. Do whatever works for you. Stephen King does not plot most of his novels and believes plotting a story is detrimental to the storytelling. John Grisham plots his stories. King believes Grisham is a great storyteller. Can you see my point? Even those who don't believe in plotting think those who plot can write good stories.

Margaret Atwood is another successful writer who does not believe in plotting. She tried it once and calls it a 'terrible mistake'.

Tom Clancy, author of *The Hunt For the Red October* and other multi-million sellers, says the most important parts of his books are 'the prime plot elements.' The type of books he writes are complex in terms of plotting, so it would be virtually impossible to come up with such stories and not bother plotting at all.

Some stories work best when plotted. There are conventions in genres of writing that would make it difficult to not plot the story, such as crime fiction. I would not call those rules, but guidelines. For a beginning novelist dabbling in crime fiction, plotting is not a dirty word. Writing a sixty-thousand-word novel can be overwhelming if you've never done it before, so having a plot to work from makes the task manageable.

Do I plot? Yes and no. Some novels I plot entirely before I write them. Other novels, I don't. I like both techniques. Literary novels don't always need detailed plotting because you are exploring the human condition, and there are endless ways to do this.

The fact is writing is a craft, and it's the end product that counts. If you've written a good story, the reader is not going to care one bit as to whether you plotted the story or not. You can write an awful novel without plotting it in advance, or you can write a great novel you've plotted. Or you can write a good novel you haven't plotted, or an awful one you have plotted. The point is you have to use whatever method works for you, whatever gets those words on paper and the story told the best way you can.

Some caution about plotting: don't spend so much time on plotting, you'll end up getting tired of the story, and by the time it comes to the writing, you just won't have the interest or passion to write it down. Write enough plot (if you choose to plot your story) so you have some idea of where the story is going.

When I plot my stories, I don't always know how they are going to end—in most cases, the ending of the story tends to work itself out be-cause of the denouement, the way the story unfolds naturally. When you plot, make sure it's the characters who seem to be pushing the plot forward, and not the other way around, otherwise the story is going to feel artificial. A well-plotted story shouldn't feel plotted. The storytelling should feel natural, and events must follow one another in a logical manner, which is why you can still write a story with a rough idea in your head, and as long as your characters are logical and consistent, you will create a plot (whether consciously or not) that should work.

Don't discuss your plot at length with every friend and family member you know. You are only going to end up confused. Keep in mind by the time you sit down to write your story, you are going to know more about it than anyone else out there. If you absolutely must share your story plot, then share it with another writer or an agent or an editor. The feedback you'll get from experts will be more valuable than from friends or family members, who in the great majority of cases do not know any-thing about solid storytelling.

So how do you actually plot a novel? There are no hard-and-fast rules about this. I used to do a chart on a large sheet of paper with my characters down the left side of the page and the events that took place at the top. Then I wrote how each character reacted to each event. It worked well for the crime novels I wrote.

For my literary novels, I prefer to write a simple two-page synopsis (a short version of the story) and use it as a guide. I give myself much more freedom with a literary novel in terms of letting the story go wherever the characters take it—pretty much like in real life, where our actions move our life 'plot' forward.

RE-WRITING & EDITING

"Whenever you feel an impulse to perpetrate a piece of exceptionally fine writing, obey it— wholeheartedly—and delete it before sending your manuscript to press. Murder your darlings."

— Sir Arthur Quiller-Couch

Anyone can write the first draft of a novel. It might be a good novel or a bad novel, but if you sit every day at your desk and add some pages to your story, you'll eventually have enough pages to call your work a novel.

The difficulty is not to write a first draft, but to end up with a publishable draft—one readers will want to read and publishers will want to buy. It's a little like playing the guitar or drawing. Many people can play guitar or draw, but not many can make a living from those because it takes considerable mastering for anyone to notice. Most people can string a sentence together, but few can bring up their writing to a publishable level, particularly with fiction. There are techniques to learn, understand and master, and these take years to achieve with confidence. For someone who reads a lot, the learning curve is shorter. For someone who seldom reads fiction (and why would such a person want to become a writer in the first place is beyond me—ego maybe?), it's going to take much longer to master the craft.

When I first began writing fiction seriously, it took me 30% of the overall time of writing a book to complete the first draft. And another 60% of my time to re-write and edit it. For example, if I wrote the first draft in one month, then it would take me another two months of revisions and re-writes before it became solid enough to be sent into the publishing world. After you've had enough experience, the first draft is getting closer to becoming the final draft. All the techniques you'll learned over the years will be incorporated into your first draft, and the second or final draft is ready for fleshing out some details and proofreading. Of course this depends on the level of complexity of your novel. A novel requiring extensive historical research means you'll end up spending much more time on the settings than if you wrote a contemporary novel set at the time and year when you are writing the story.

This is where good grammar comes into it, and I have discussed this at length in a previous chapter, so I will not repeat myself here. Your re-writing consists of several aspects, but not limited to those depending on what genre you are writing in and the skills you have already acquired in writing fiction:

- spelling and grammar corrections;
- sensory details flesh-out (smell, sound, taste, sight and touch);
- consistency check (character details, settings and so on);
- dialogue check;
- paragraphing;
- style.

I'm sure other professional writers would be able to add to this list, but this book is not about techniques. There are plenty of other good books out there in the market. This is more of a guide to let you know what you are in for, and to spell out strongly how re-writing is a very important aspect of writing, and some writers would even argue 're-writing' is in fact writing. The writing becomes good after you've done a re-write. The majority of first drafts are bad, and professional writers know this is the case, hence why they do not share their first drafts with anyone. Negative criticism after showing your first draft can lead you to feel as if you don't have what it takes to write a novel, so it's best to soldier on before sharing your work until you've done a draft solid enough to pass around.

DIALOGUE

"When dialogue is right, we know. When it's wrong we also know—it jags on the ear like a badly tuned musical instrument."

—Stephen King

Dialogue is an important part of the novel, and yet some novels are published with virtually no dialogue. My novel *The Suffering* has no dialogue for roughly the first quarter of the novel. This is done on purpose to highlight the way people can be lonely after a break-up and don't talk to anyone for days. However, because of television and films, readers are used to dialogue, and they expect it in novels, particularly genre novels and contemporary novels. Readers are impatient and want stories to move fast. It doesn't mean you have to do this if your story doesn't call for it. It means you need to be aware this is what readers prefer, and a slower book means fewer readers. I'm not overly concerned with this because I write firstly for the story, and then hopefully find some readers who will enjoy it.

The usage of dialogue in novels is not a gimmick. Just like in real life, dialogue between characters reveals who they are, what they think and how they react to a situation. Dialogue also helps to maintain dramatic tension between characters since the basis of drama is conflict, and conflict leads to argumentative dialogue.

What is good dialogue?

Dialogue is good when you don't notice it and it blends in with the narrative of the story. Good dialogue ping-pongs from one character to another. People do not speak in long monologues, but in some novels you can get away with it, although you have to be careful you do not use dialogue to reveal too much exposition, particularly back story and technical exposition, or the dialogue is going to end up sounding stilted.

Here's a sample of fast dialogue from *The Suffering*. In this scene, we have a young woman who self-abuses and is forced to meet with a psychiatrist on a weekly basis:

He says, "The less you say, the longer this is going to take."
She stares at him a little longer. "What do you want to know?"
"You can begin by telling me about those scratches on your arms."
The bastard has seen the cuts.
Valérie plays with the sleeve ending of her jumper. "Okay, but this is going to sound worse than it really is..."
"Tell me."
She hesitates. "I..."
Dr Keener stares at her, clearly expecting some kind of explanation.
"I don't need to tell you—it's totally irrelevant," she says.
"Why are you hurting yourself?"
Valérie leans back on her chair. "Long story—"
"—we've got a whole hour."
"It's going to take longer than an hour."
"We'll resume next week. Nothing is rushing us."
"Okay, my girlfriend is no longer with me..."
"And?"
"The scratching is a way to deal with the pain—it helps me cope."

In this example, the characters are reacting to what the other one is saying, which is how dialogue should be. Each have an agenda, and the agendas clash. He wants to find out why she harms herself, and she just wants to get it all over and done with and get her weekly prescription pills. The result is a tug-of-war with the dialogue, which also reveals information about the two characters. There are no long sentences here, but just interaction between both characters.

There are other ways to write dialogue, of course. Some dialogue is constructed with much longer sentences, and it can work.

In some of Patricia Cornwell's novels, some of the characters have monologues lasting an entire page. This serves the story because those characters tend to explain in detail a forensic or crime theory or scientific explanation essential to the plot. However, you really need to be careful here if choosing to do the same in your novel, and you must ensure the dialogue sounds natural. Read it out loud. Does it sound like someone talking?

learning to write dialogue

What's the best way to learn how to write dialogue? Read novels you love and study the dialogue. Another way, which I found to be quite effective, is to read screenplays, which are filled with dialogue, particularly comedies and sitcoms. Have a go at writing screenplay scenes, and this will help you to develop your dialogue skills.

Nowadays, it's best to use a software when dabbling into screenplay writing. The most common and popular ones are Movie Magic and Final Draft, but I prefer a little-known British one called Movie Draft, which is clutter-free and very affordable compared to the popular ones.

Dialogue is not conversation. In real life we chit-chat with people we know, and we talk about trivial things. In novels, there is no time for chit-chat. Dialogue is there for a specific purpose, and one of the major reasons is to maintain dramatic conflict. Even if you have two characters involved in a civilized conversation, make sure they are still arguing a little about something. This creates automatic dramatic tension, and it will make readers want to continue reading.

Readers are attracted to conflict, and when you have conflicting situations in a novel, they want to read on.

Dialogue is also good when explaining scientific details. Instead of having long paragraphs of explanations, like you might find in a crime novel, one character could simply be explaining the details to another.

Good dialogue also adds colour to characters. Someone from a low-social, economic back-ground will not talk the same as a British aristocrat, and your dialogue should reflect this, otherwise your characters will feel contrived and unrealistic.

Dialogue can also be used to advance plot and move the story forward. What one character says to another can trigger a new action, which forces the plot forward. When this is done with skill, readers will not notice how dialogue is constructed and will want to read on.

How do you know how much dialogue is needed? It depends on the genre you are writing in, and on the style you prefer. As previously mentioned, some novels have very little dialogue in them, particularly literary novels. Hard-boiled crime fiction, on the other hand, depends heavily on dialogue, and hence you must have a good mastery of dialogue technique to get away with it.

Once you've figured out the novel genre you want to write, study similar published books and work out how much dialogue is in them. Photocopy some pages and highlight the dialogue sections. This will give you a good estimate of how much is required.

Each scene with dialogue should start with some sort of conflict, debate and conclusion, which should lead to new action and further debates.

THE CRAFT OF FICTION

"I think the story compels its own style to a great extent, that the writer don't need to bother too much about style. If he's bothering about style, then he's going to write precious emptiness—not necessarily nonsense…it'll be quite beautiful and quite pleasing to the ear, but there won't be much content in it."

—William Faulkner

Fiction is the ability to make readers believe how what you have written actually happened (or is happening if you choose to write in the present tense), but it's really all made up. And don't start telling me it has really happened, so it's a non-fiction novel. There is no such thing as a non-fiction novel, and yet I have heard novice writers refer to this non-existing genre throughout the years. A novel inspired by true events is still fiction. What the writer has done is invented scenes and dialogue. It's not a word-for-word account of what truly happened. If a writer chooses to write a biography or memoir, then it's non-fiction.

Your job as a writer is to make the world in the novel feel as real as the world around us, but you need to dramatize everything otherwise readers will fall asleep. Real life is not as dramatic, and if it were, we would all end up in hospital with a nervous breakdown.

One of my writing students once complained how all

stories are just 'fish-out-of-water' stories. He was right, but this is the nature of fiction. Something happens to someone (the pro-tagonist); that person is forced to react; there are opposite forces; that person keeps on fighting; and then you have an ending. It doesn't matter if you write literary fiction or genre fiction, this is the most basic premise of all fiction. It works because it creates instant conflict, and conflict is the essence of all drama. Recall your favorite novels and movies, and you'll see they are all 'fish-out-of-water' scenarios. There is no way around this structure I am aware of.

When readers pick up a novel, they expect to be faced with a fish-out-of-water scenario, even if they are not aware of it. Their past experience with novel reading means they are conditioned to expect novels to tell stories about a person or a group of people who are forced to react to something, hence the fish-out-of-water scenario.

The craft of fiction is to use this device, find an interesting theme (or several themes) to explore and create a story so real to readers, they will feel they have lived another person's life when they have finished reading the novel. This is known as suspension of disbelief—readers know they are reading fiction, but they are willing to accept the world you have created even though they know it's not real. If you do your job well, the world you have created will feel as real as real life.

But what if you write science-fiction or fantasy? The same rules apply. Good fiction is good fiction, irrespective of the genre. If you use sensory details, do good research and master the techniques of fiction, you can create an invented setting. Which will feel as real to readers as the world they live in.

SELF-PUBLISHING

"The good news about self publishing is you get to do everything yourself. The bad news about self publishing is you get to do everything yourself."

—Lori Lesko

The game has now changed forever since the invention of digital technology and the Internet. Writers can choose to release their work to worldwide markets and not bother with traditional publishers. The debate of traditional vs self-publishing is endless because both methods are proven effective and suitable for all types of writers.

Traditional publishing can offer good advances, good publicity and the opportunity to be financially secure—for bestselling authors, that is. In reality, very few novelist make a living from writing novels, but it doesn't mean it's impossible. A traditional publisher also tends to take care of all the aspects of publishing so you can focus on the writing. If you are successful, however, you will be expected to produce one book a year and spend the rest of the time promoting it. If your books sell to countries around the world, you could make a good income.

The reality is the greater majority of first time novels never get published by traditional publishers. The statistics are something like ten first time novels are published for every five-thousand unsolicited manuscripts received.

That's where self-publishing can overcome the odds. With Amazon's Kindle and Create-Space, two of the many platforms available for self-publishing, you can have your book published and released to the world in only a few days. Does it work? Yes and no. Over 80% of all books published in 2014 were self-published or independently published books (small publishers, or writers running their own small presses). Most self-published books make around $100 per year, and the money is made from writers buying copies of their own books (which can be turned into profit if they sell them). But, there have been cases of self-published authors who have done really well because of the topic they've chosen and their ability to write solidly and professionally. Kerry Wilkinson in the UK sold 250,000 copies of his self-published crime fiction in the last quarter of 2011, beating every author, even those published commercially. He promoted the book through his own website and social networking, something many self-published authors cannot be bothered doing. It's a lot of work, and Wilkinson said if he was offered a traditional publishing contract, he would take it up.

So why would you self publish if your book is not going to sell hundreds of thousands of copies like Wilkinson?

There are a few reasons why you would want to choose self-publishing as an option to traditional publishing. The first one is you do not want to wait years for your book to find a home. The second is you don't like the terms and conditions of traditional publishers. The third is you want to keep rights to your books entirely. The fourth is you can test the market before sending your book to traditional publishers. The fifth is you have not been successful with traditional publishers, which means you haven't wasted years writing for nothing. And the sixth is a published book is good for your career if your are working in academia or any field where having a book published gives you credibility and a better chance for promotion.

Should you self-publish or not? There are no right and wrong answers here, and it really depends where you stand in life in terms of your fiction and what type of success you want. There are no guarantees of success either way.

An effective way to test the market with your new novel is to release it on Kindle only and under a pseudonym. Give some free copies during a promotion period and see what readers think. Expect some ridiculous feedback from readers who are illiterate (and you can tell because their feedback is filled with spelling an grammatical errors), which you can choose to freely ignore. However, if you get nothing but one-star ratings, you're clearly doing something wrong. Using a pseudonym will protect your reputation if your book is not as good as you thought it might have been.

Some traditional publishers will also not look at self-published, so if you find your book is rated highly by readers, you can remove it from Kindle, change the title, put your name on it, and send it with confidence to traditional publishers. Be aware it does not guarantee a traditional publisher will pick it up, and it could be years before you see it in print again. This is what you need to decide, and there is not really a ready-made solution for this dilemma. It's a personal decision based on your needs, and what you hope to achieve with your career.

There are writers who have given up completely on traditional publishers because they don't like the deals, contracts, or the hassles of having to negotiate with them. They also like to have full control of their creative output. Anything written can be published, and no one can tell them whether a manuscript should be published or not.

If successful with self-publishing, you can make more money than with a traditional publisher. For example, Amazon though its Kindle Self Publishing program offers up to 70%

royalty on the retail price, which is way above the 10% offered by traditional publishers. To make the same amount of money you would with a traditional publisher, you only have sell around 1/7 of the books (if they are both at the same retail price). It's clear looking at those figures how Wilkinson would have made a significant return on his writing investment.

Another writer who's worth noticing is the author of *Sideways,* Rex Pickett, whose film adaptation of the novel won an academy award for Best Writing, Screenplay Based on Material from Another Medium. Pickett doesn't believe that the traditional publishing platform is going to remain alive for much longer:

"I predict in less than 10 years time, the traditional publishing industry, now moribund and flailing like a bird on broken wings, will be dead, or will morph into something almost totally unrecognizable from what it was for a century."

Pickett believes the industry is so messed up, publishers don't care about their authors any longer. He ended up self-publishing *Vertical (Sideways 2)* and *Chile (Sideways 3)* because of his professional frustration with traditional publishers. The original *Sideways* novel was rejected countless times before it was made into a movie, and then sold for an advance of only $5000. Pickett found the whole publishing experience with traditional publishers so annoying and deceitful that he chose to not bother with them anymore. As a result of the success of the film version, he is well-enough known to make self-publishing work for him.

He adds in the Huffington Post, "When people meet me and learn that I wrote *Sideways* they're shocked to find out I'm not a multimillionaire. Not even close, I inform them. In fact I'm a bona fide member of the 99%. The 99% of authors who were royally screwed over by the traditional publishing world, in my case (a) St. Martin's Press, and then (b), Alfred A. Knopf. Screwed over by ignorance, nearsightedness, and, in the latter case, mistreatment of an established author that bordered on fraud and contractual misconduct."

This, of course, does not mean it's going to happen to you, but you need to be aware of what can go wrong when someone else is in charge of your publishing output. You have no say in what, when and how (unless you're are Stephen King or similar).

If you want to avoid the type of frustration detailed here by Pickett, self-publishing might be a better option for your career.

There are many e-publishing platforms out there, but Kindle and CreateSpace are free and the most cost-effective way to publish your work without financial losses. So it's basically true you can make money without spending any if you know how to write and edit your work, and typeset it for Kindle or CreateSpace. Watch out for sharks out there who charge a lot of money just to convert your book to an e-book. Every time new technology appears, someone is trying to rip-off those who have creative ambitions.

Self-publishing and small press publishing are no longer dirty words like they were for decades, and this is now your chance to be in charge of your writing career if you choose to. The red tape is gone, and the only attributes required are your talent, passion, dedication and enthusiasm. There is a whole generation of readers who don't differentiate between traditional and inde-pendent publishing. They just want good books to read, and where they come from and who publishes them is of no concern to those readers.

The ball is in your court.

GENRE WRITING

"Good writing is good writing. In many ways, it's the audience and their expectations that define a genre. A reader of literary fiction expects the writing to illuminate the human condition, some aspect of our world and our role in it. A reader of genre fiction likes that, too, as long as it doesn't get in the way of the story."

—Rosemary Clement-Moore

There is a real display of snobbery from those who only read literature and dismiss genre fiction as hack writing. This whole attitude is totally nonsense in my view because, as I have previously mentioned, good writing is good writing, irrespective of the genre.

Nonetheless, you will find yourself at times having to deal with narrow-minded people who regard genre writers as Neanderthal. The best thing to do is to avoid them like the plague.

I don't believe one genre of writing is superior or inferior to another. As an author, I write crime novels, thrillers, non-fiction and literature. My crime novels and literary novels have won international awards in the USA, Europe and Australia. In terms of writing, it's all the same to me. I can appreciate literature and genre fiction. Sometimes I choose a theme that cannot be explored through a crime book, and only literature will do. And sometimes it's the other way around.

As a writer, your goal—once you have chosen a theme and

story line—is to decide which genre is going to serve the story best. If you choose a theme that deals with the relationship between a mother and a teenage daughter, it's more likely literature is going to serve the story better than genre fiction. Or maybe young adult fiction if you choose to write the story from the daughter's viewpoint.

For obvious reasons, a story based on a true crime event will be served better in the crime and mystery genre. Some stories work well as a mixture of two genres, such as James Lee Burke's Robicheaux novels, which are arguably literary crime fiction. Burke comes from a literary background and tried crime fiction when a friend told him it was easier to get a publishing contract for a crime writer than a literary writer. What he ended up doing is grafting his literary style into the crime genre and came up with a hybrid genre, which made his work somewhat unique in the world of crime fiction.

The lesson here is how by restricting ourselves to the reading of one genre only, we are also limiting what is possible in terms of fiction writing. The more we are open to all genres of fiction, the more potentially creative we are in terms of varying and challenging our writing techniques.

Write what pleases you, first and foremost, irrespective of what others think, and if you do a good job, you will find readers who will appreciate your work.

CROSS-GENDER WRITING

"The point is, it's not impossible to find good female characters in male writers' books. It's just much harder than it should be."

—Ester Bloom

There will come a time during your fiction writing when you will wonder what it is like to write a novel from the opposite sex. You might have a good theme and a story, but suddenly find the best way to tell this story is from the opposite gender. If you're a male writer, this means you could write a novel from a female viewpoint, and if you're a female writer, from a male's viewpoint. Wally Lamb has done this very successfully with his novel *She Come Undone*. He tells the story from a woman's viewpoint, but at no stage during the story does it feel as if a man has written the story. Lamb spent decades teaching at high school, and he understood young people and women particularly well, hence the reason why he managed to pull off so successfully a woman's viewpoint in his first-person-narrated novel.

Whatever the reason, writing with a narrator from the opposite sex forces you to see the world through a set of different eyes. It's certainly challenging if you've never done it, but it can also be rewarding.

I have written from the opposite sex several times and

found the experience liberating. It got me out of my head for a while and offered me the chance to explore ideas and situations I have not been able to experience in real life. Lamb said after he had written *She's Come Undone*, he understood women better than before he started working on the project.

If you are going to write from the opposite sex viewpoint, I suggest you read at least half a dozen—but twice as much would be better— novels where the narrator is the same as the one you intend. This will give a solid idea of how the opposite sex thinks. For example, it is well-known how men in general think more 'visually' when it comes to women, whilst women think more 'emotionally'. Of course, this is a general rule, not an absolute, but if you want your narrator to 'feel' realistic, you need to keep this in mind.

Whilst gender makes us different, our humanity is the same. We share the same need for love, and the same emotions—lust, fear, hate, admiration, jealousy, greed. By tapping into the 'truth' of your human emotions, you will be able to feel convincingly from the opposite sex.

Some writers write from two different viewpoints in a single novel, normally altering from one chapter to the other. *The Pillow Fight* by Matthew Condo shifts from a male's perspective to a female's perspective in every chapter. The book also turns the victim-abuser on its head by making the physically violent abuser the female, and the recipient of the abuse a male. To be able to do this, the author had to really get into the characters' heads and see what it would be like to be those characters.

One of the problems you can encounter when cross-gender writing is having a female narrator when the author of the novel is male, or a male narrator when the author of the novel if female. It means some readers will purposely try to find errors in the book and claim the authenticity of the narrator is at doubt because the author is not a man or woman and could never really understand what it's like to be one or the other.

This undermines the fact we can understand and sympathize with the opposite sex without being 'one of them'. Since I have mentioned before we all experience the same emotions, it is possible to switch gender when writing and do it convincingly.

I've solved this problem twice by publishing my books under the name of a gender which is not the same as mine, and the reviewers never said anything about the 'gender' issue because the name of the author matched the gender of the narrator. One of those books, published under a woman's pseudonym, won an interna-tional book award for Best Sequel.

A CREATIVE PARTNER

"When you have a writing partner and you're writing a comedy, your goal is to make each other laugh."

—Lauren Miller

Unless you want to spend the rest of your life like a hermit, I will assume at some stage you might decide to go out there and find the person you will spend a good amount of your life with. I have been with my partner for over twenty-years now, and she's a writer too. It has been good because the common interest we have in writing and reading has made it easier to keep the relationship going during difficult periods. When we talk to one another, we actually have something of interest to the both of us. We spend a lot of time talking about writing, publishing, storytelling, other writers, writing courses and so on. I think if my partner wasn't into writing, the relationship wouldn't have lasted as long.

Is it a necessity to partner with another writer? No, obviously not all writers are married or attached to another writer. But I do believe if you are going to spend years or even decades with one person, you would do well to choose a creative person. It doesn't necessarily have to be a writer—even a painter or a musician is more likely to understand your crea-tive needs. People who are not creative don't always understand creativity, and they tend to see creative people as big kids who haven't grown up. They also tend to treat your vocation as a hobby until you make some serious money out of it.

I'm not suggesting you run away from the love of your life because this person is not creative, but if you have a choice, then put yourself in a situation where you meet creative people, and this way you are more likely to fall for someone who is also creative.

The counter-argument to this is if you partner with someone who is not a creative person but makes a solid and steady income, enough for two, then you can really indulge in getting your writing career on the fast-track. This is not a bad position to be in because as we have previously seen, the majority of novelists cannot live only on the income derived from fiction writing, and you'll have the security of a solid income to fall back on without having hours of your creative time being stripped away from you. By no means, am I suggesting here you become a gold digger and only aim for people who have money. At the end of the day, being with someone for a long time should have something to do with love and respect. What I am suggesting is you place yourself in environments that will help you to fall in love with someone who is more likely to be supportive of your creative ambitions and hope-fully someone who is financially stable enough so you don't have to worry about the roof over your head or digging trenches for a living while you slave away on that first novel.

For the record, I have quite a few creative friends who were not attached to creative people, and it never worked out. They ended up separating because the non-creative type didn't *get* them, and they just didn't understand why the writer wanted to spend so much time by themselves in a room in front of a laptop. It becomes a tug-of-war between the writing and the partner. The more time you spend by yourself writing, the less time you spend with the other person. And it gets to a point where it become *me or the writing*. You do not want to tie yourself with someone who asks you to abandon your life goal so you can spend more time watching evening television together on a couch and become creatively deprived to the point of insanity.

If, however, you do end up with a partner who is not creative but passionate about something, then encourage your partner to really indulge in his passion. Even if your partner is a working person, but he loves sport, for example, encourage him to join a sport association and to take it seriously. I do believe relationships can last longer when both partners are passionate about something and are actively involved in it. They are less likely to argue about not spending enough time together and become bored with one another.

In conclusion, I'm not a psychologist, but I do believe as a writer, you need to make the right choices in life if you want to climb this mountain and not give up halfway through because of the attitude of another person.

And if your partner is psychologically and physically abusive every time you choose to write, run as fast as you can.

MONEY

"A prose fiction writer's hourly wage, broken down into units, would be in the modest range of the US minimum wage of the 1950s – approximately $1 per hour."

—Joyce Carol Oates

It would be irresponsible to tackle a book on what it's like to be a novelist without mentioning money.

Early on, I did mention how the greater majority of novelists do not make enough money from their books to make a living. This applies even more to literary novelists because the books sell in lower numbers.

Whether we like it or not, the world revolves around money, and money is time, and you give your time for money so you can have a roof over your head and eat.

The downside to this is you might be forced to do something you don't like just to survive—and let's face it, this how it is for the majority of people out there.

So how do you make enough money to live on and still find the time to write your novels?

In the previous chapter, I suggested how one way is to fall in love with someone who is financially stable, and who is happy to provide for two or even for the whole family if you have children. One of you needs at least a steady job and income, otherwise it will be difficult.

You basically have two ways to make enough money to live on. The first is to work for a maximum hourly rate with minimum time at work. If you can get away with working around ten hours per week and still make a full time income, you'll have plenty of time to get the writing done.

How is this possible?

I teach creative writing at university, and I get paid very good money for it. As a result I only work six to ten hours per week and receive the equivalent of a full salary of a semi-professional worker. My partner, who is also a writer, works as an academic in writing at a university, and brings in enough money on her side to make our lives comfortable.

I suggested earlier on, when discussing the advantages and disadvantages of studying creative writing at university, how if you insist on gaining a degree, you might be better off doing a course that has nothing to do with writing, but which knowledge you'll be able to use in your creative work. If you've decided to go down such a path, choose a job you are somewhat interested in, and which has good job opportunities once you have graduated. Do some research first. Check the classified adver-tisements. You don't want to have to do an entire second degree because you were not careful in choosing the right one in the first place. Let's look again at John Grisham and Michael Crichton. Grisham is a lawyer, and without his law degree and his experience in the the legal profession, he would have never written the novels he wrote, and we most likely would have never heard of him. Crichton is a medical doctor and worked in a hospital emergency department. This is where he got the idea of ER, one of the most successful television dramas of all times. His interest in anything scientific forged his career as a novelist by blending scientific knowledge and research and resulted in the writing of *Jurassic Park*, *The Lost World* and tens of other novels, which use science as the main plotting device in this stories.

Robin Cook is a doctor who made millions from writing

nothing but medical thrillers. He could have never done this if he had not studied medicine.

Patricia Cornwell, who was brought up in a dysfunctional family, did a degree in English and worked as a crime reporter for the *Charlotte Observer*. Later on, she worked as a technical writer and computer analyst for the Office of the Chief Medical Examiner in Virginia and volunteered for the Richmond Police Depart-ment. Without her studies and background, she would have not written the Scarpetta series of novels, which have sold millions worldwide.

My point is you don't need to focus on just writing in your life. You have to have something to write about. Because we live in a world where money is necessary for survival, you'll most likely have to pick a 'side-job' in addition to your writing vocation. So make sure you choose something you are fascinated with, preferably as much as you are with writing, be it law, medicine police work, or anything else but creative writing itself.

Now, if you have absolutely no interest in anything else, then by all means, undertake a MFA in writing and teach writing at university or junior college. It worked for me and my partner, and we are making a comfortable living from teaching creative writing whilst we continue to work as novelists. This is not accidental and was part of the career plan we made in our early twenties. We were aware of the difficulty in making an income solely from fiction writing, so we choose as our side career something involving writing, hence we studied writing at university in order to be qualified to teach others. We had no other real interest and felt it best if we just remain in the writing community, even if the books didn't pay the mortgage.

Some novelists prefer to work in menial jobs because those jobs are not mentally taxing, and they choose to use their mental energy for writing. This can work, obviously, but the downside is you have to put in quite a lot of hours to make ends meet, and very often a low-wage menial job is not enough, and you'll find yourself having to work at another job on top, leaving you very little time to do any writing at all.

I do believe it's best when you are young, debt free and with no children to get a solid education as soon as possible before life gets in the way, and you are too busy making ends meet to study anything.

However, a word of caution: be very careful your 'second' ambition does not take over the first one. It's meant to be a way to support your writing, not the main job, and if you find you are no longer writing, it means you have chosen a side career that demands too much of your free time and leaves you no time to write fiction.

If you absolutely have to make a living from something other than writing, which most of us novelists do, then a professional job with part-time hours will work best. You will get the writing done.

One final word here: unemployment benefits. Most successful artists have at one time or another had to rely on unemployment benefits in order to avoid starvation and living in the streets. Use this as a last resort, but whilst you are not working, make sure you write as much as possible. Don't squander the free time you've been given. To save money, use your local library and you'll save on power bills (as I have discussed in a previous chapter).

If you rely on unemployment benefits during the writing of your novel, it might be a good idea to share a home with others as it will lower your share of rent considerably. It will also cut down on the cost of food and utilities.

CHILDREN

"You look at the finished book and you think, 'Oh damn it, I should have changed that.' You're never happy. Whereas with a baby, you're happy. If you've got a perfect baby, you're just grateful."

—J.K. Rowlings

Children can be a blessing on a curse. If you have kids around the house all day, it's pretty hard to concentrate on writing your novel because they need so much attention and care. On the other hand, once they are old enough to go to school, you'll have plenty of time to write in the mornings and the afternoons.

Having children means in some countries and states you are allowed to have parents' financial assistance of some sort from the government. If you are a single parent, you normally get an equivalent of the unemployment benefit, which is not nearly enough to make a living, but with a part-time job on the side, you could have enough time to write your novel. If you have to rely on a parent's pension to live on, then you might want to consider living in a rural area where rents and housing are relatively cheap, and where your dollar will go further. In big cities, the biggest expense is housing, particularly renting where there is no rent-controlled housing.

Children can also be a great inspiration for your own work. Some successful novelists have ended up writing children's books because of being surrounded by their own children and finding the motivation to write stories for them.

I have a friend who is a published novelist and children books writer who used to hire a babysitter when she did her writing. This gave her two solid hours of writing a day when she was never disturbed. Her husband was a psychiatrist, so the money he took home was enough for the whole family and paying a babysitter. It worked for her, and she published two novels and five children's books during those two solid hours of writing.

Jennifer Weiner, author of *Goodnight Nobody*, has some advise for writing mothers:

"If you're a mom, get yourself some help and some time. I'm incredibly lucky that I can afford a good nanny. But you could also set up a baby-sitting co-op with a friend who wants to do something for herself. Or get some time from your spouse or partner. Time is such an important thing, it's elusive."

Some parents say one day when the kids are gone, they will start writing. The risk here is they will no longer have the motivation, and they will also be years behind in terms of learning the craft. The earlier you start to learn how to write fiction, and the longer you keep at it, the better you will be as the years go by. If you start writing at forty, you'll be already twenty years behind those who have begun writing at twenty and not stopped since then.

It's important to write a little every single day, even if it's just one hour. Kids normally go to bed before adults, so this could mean writing one hour before going to bed yourself, or it could mean getting up one hour earlier than anyone else in the household and getting on with the writing.

Micheal Chabon, author of *Wonder Boys*, has three children and would rather spend time with his family when they are awake than writing. So he sets his writing schedule from 10 p.m. to 4 a.m., from Sunday until Thursday. This sounds like a difficult way to write, but it works for him. As a parent you need to find what works for you rather than make excuses for not writing.

Whatever you decide to do, you need to make time for the writing and make writing a habit, otherwise you are going to end up being just another person who wishes she were a writer. Don't use your kids as a reason to not do any writing. You will be angry at them, and you're just really finding an excuse to not get the work done instead of finding ways to make it work for yourself.

Weiner adds, "I spend part of my day as a mom, and part of my day as a writer, and it really works well for me."

It's all about managing the time you have and ensuring some of it is spent writing on a daily basis.

The writing doesn't happen by itself.

You have to find the time to write.

THE YOUNG WRITER

"The question one asks of the young writer who wants to know if he's got what it takes is this: "Is writing novels what you want to do? Really want to do?" If the young writer answers, "Yes," then all one can say is: Do it. In fact, he will anyway."

—John Garner

If you are a young writer and still live with your parents, don't leave home, especially if your parents are agreeable to live with. You might never get a chance again to live rent-free, and in some cases be fed and clothed for next to nothing. This is now the time to take the writing seriously and to really hammer everything you can into it. Once you leave your parents' home, you will be financially responsible for yourself, and this means having to get a job and less time to write.

In the old days, writers had patrons of the arts who gave them money just to write. Some people had way too much money, and others had a lot of talent, so it worked for everyone.

These days are gone. The only money you are going to see from your writing are royalties, government grants, writing prizes and, if you are lucky, an advance of some sort. It is very difficult to keep your head above water and be creative when you're broke, can't pay the gas bill and can't feed yourself.

If your parents don't kick you out of home, then don't

move out. Be very productive with the time you have and write. If your parents are artists, they will understand this and most likely accept to support you as long as *you write!*

Now, if you are going to continue living at your parents' home as an adult, do something for them in return. Don't use your parents as doormats and clean up after yourself. It's not about sucking up, but about being smart and grateful in terms of what you've been given, and it's also as a sign of respect for those who believe in you enough to let you stay past your mid-twenties and don't treat you like a child who is never going to grow up.

In terms of feeding oneself, there are plenty of soup kitchens around most cities, so grab your worst clothes possible and turn up. If you're broke and can't afford to feed yourself, guess what? You're not faking it!

Collect food discount coupons, those offering food at fifty percent off and so on. Look for the specials at supermarkets. Shop at the fresh produce market. It's cheaper than your standard supermarket food. If you share a home with others, then sharing meals is also much cheaper than cooking for one.

Of course, the ultimate sponging is to find a partner who has a regular job and is willing to support you whilst you're writing those novels. It's not a far-fetched idea, and many now-successful writer made it by sponging on others. The wife or husband support them for a couple of years or more, and then the writers made enough money for two. If your partner believes you have talent, then it is totally possible to achieve. Your partner is investing in you. But you cannot sit at home all day and watch television. You've made a pact. The love of your life supports you financially, and in return you write and try the hardest to make some money from the writing.

If you are on your own, it's tougher because you are fully responsible for your well-being. If you like comfort, I suggest renting a room in a house with all the comforts. For a fraction of the cost of a rent, you'll have your own room to write in and not struggle with paying utility bills and the likes. Some rooms include all utilities in the rent, so you know exactly what your expenses are going to be for the week. Some houses also include one or two meals a day, so you won't even have to worry about cooking.

As a writer, it's also a good idea to have a few good friends when you are still struggling financially. I am not suggesting here you borrow money from them (it's a sure way to ensure they won't remain friends for long), but don't hesitate in accepting dinner invitations on a regular basis. Fourteen friends means two weeks of free dinners. You can pay them back when you become a bestselling author, if you happen to be one of those lucky few, and pay off their mortgages as a thank-you. There are some people in society who are delighted in helping struggling artists because they either admire creativity or wish they were artists themselves but don't have what it takes (which is usually a combination of time, talent and persistence).

Another way to minimize your expenses is to barter your services for a roof. Not everything has to be traded with money. Maybe there is an elderly person who lives in a mansion but cannot do the house maintenance required, so for the return of a free room and board, you do the maintenance. You might even be offered a small stipend on top of it all, enough to buy some wine and go to the movies now and then.

As a young writer, you need to be careful of two things—over confidence and doubt. I have come across many cocky, young writers who believed themselves to be geniuses when in fact the quality of their work was below average. Being arrogant during the early stages of your writing career means you will build a resistance to change and learning. Only when you can see the weaknesses in your writing, you will improve.

The other side of the coin is those new writers who are forever paralyzed by self-doubt, who keep on comparing their work to those of masters and chastised themselves for not being up to their levels. As a new novelist, you are in you apprentice stage of your career, so it's impossible for you to be writing at the same level as the masters. Once you realize this and accept it, you are less likely to be anxious about your work, and just get on with it.

You wouldn't expect an apprentice carpenter to be at the same level as a master carpenter, so why expect your writing to be at the same level as a successful published writer? It's deceptive and can leave you feeling talent-less and running out of stamina.

Write the best fiction you can and keep writing and learning. It's all you can do. No amount of self-doubt or arrogance is going to improve your writing. Focus on the craft, not the self, and you are more likely to end up with the skills required to produce good fiction.

WHEN IS IT TIME TO GIVE UP?

"If you're a writer, your first duty, a duty you owe to yourself and your readers, and to your writing itself, is to become wonderful. To become the best writer you can possibly be."

—Theodora Goss

The answer is *never*.

I repeat: *never*. The moment you have set your heart on becoming a novelist is the moment you must stick to it until you drop dead, otherwise you're just selling your soul to the devil.

The most important ingredient for an artist, be it a writer, an actor, a painter or a musician is persistence—beyond anything. Persistence with the writing, with the learning of the craft, with trying different techniques, with getting the work published. There is nothing more depressing than giving up on a goal you have been working on for ten or twenty years because then you'd have basically wasted a good chunk of your life achieving less than nothing. The moment you give up is the moment you will never make it—period. Books won't be written, your craft will not improve and nobody will buy a non-published book.

If you feel never giving up is not for you, please don't even start a career as a novelist, and save yourself the headache and disap-pointment. At this stage, I would like to recommend *Youth* by John Coetzee, a work of fiction, which is really based on the author's observations. It's a story about how to screw up your life as an artist (in the book, the artist is a poet, but this applies equally well to novelists and other artists). It's a big moral lesson and one worth exploring, even if it's delivered in the form of fiction. The lesson is about side-tracking and not writing anymore, and seeing your dreams vanish forever because of your own limitations in terms of persistence and passion. For a would-be-novelist or any artist, it's a must-read because it stresses how you have to persist with the craft and never give up, no matter what.

There are plenty of successful writers nowadays who had great odds stacked against them and persisted for years before anything concrete happened in their writing lives. If they had given up before they reached the point where the writing was solid and wanted by publishers and readers, they would have never made it. Out of all these writers, there are undoubtedly a greater number who have given up, and whom we will never hear about.

An artist's life is meant to be difficult. You are going against the grain. The world is not waiting for you to write a book. The world is not going to miss the book you have yet to write. The world doesn't really need another book. So if you must write, then be sincere as to why you are writing. It has to come from passion and the desire to write more than anything else. It has to be like the breath you are taking in. You cannot stop breathing or you will die.

And if you are a real writer, you cannot stop writing, or your soul will die.

When is it time to give up?

Never.

THE PLEASURE OF WRITING

"To me, the greatest pleasure of writing is not what it's about, but the inner music that words make."

—Truman Capote

Writers write for all kind of reasons, and it's now widely accepted creative writing has some therapeutic benefits (you can even do a Master of Science in Creative Writing for Therapeutic Purposes accredited by Middlesex University in the UK), and many writers just enjoy the process of writing for the sake of the writing itself, not necessarily because the work will get published or make money.

'...whilst is no panacea, some writers find its practice therapeutic; and some teachers of writing believe that writing is a powerful aid to various types of therapy, from the treatment of depression to social rehabilitation.' (The Cambridge Introduction to Creative Writing, p. 3).

Creative writing is also linked to self-development and self-awareness.

Yet, western society is obsessed with linking creative writing with publishing and making money. There is nothing wrong with making money from what you love doing, but it shouldn't be the beginning and ending of it all. You do not have to write and shouldn't write for the sole purpose of deriving an income, certainly not when writing fiction.

If you play tennis or football on the weekends, no one expects you to become professional at it. It's fine to just enjoy doing those activities, and yet, with creative writing, you are constantly judged on whether you are published or not. There is nothing wrong with writing for the sheer enjoyment of writing, and with all those self-publishing platforms out there, you can still make your work available to the world even if you don't want to be involved with the business side of publishing, or deal directly with publishers. Creative writing can remain a hobby, the same as golf, tennis, football, swimming, poker playing and hundreds of other activities. You can live in your own cocoon of creative writing without having to justify what you are doing to anyone.

Some writers purposely avoid the com-mercialization of their work. They are more interested in producing good work.

Mark Winegardner was selected to write the sequel to Puzo's *Godfather* but he faced the challenge of writing up to the phenomenal bestseller published before his.

'Puzo said he was trying to grow up and sell out. I was trying to do the opposite—I was trying to grow up and not sell out. I wasn't trying to write a bestseller; I wrote it to be a good book.'

He could have easily used formulaic writing in order to ensure the book sells, but he was acutely aware of the importance of quality and refused to focus on writing a bestseller.

THE OLDER WRITER

"It's never too late to be who you might have been."

—George Elliot

Writers come in all shapes and sizes and *ages*. It's not uncommon for new writers to be past their forties or fifties. After a lifetime of work and other commitments, some people decide to become writers because they had always wanted to do it for years, or because they've decided this is what they want to do now. Either way, beginning writing when you are older has its advantages and drawbacks.

Let's begin with the drawbacks. If you start to get into creative writing later in life, you'll have already lost a few decades of fine-tuning and mastering the craft of fiction. It will take you years to master it, so you'll need to really focus on what you are doing. You'll find some people half your age might write fiction better than you do because they have been doing it for much longer. You risk becoming more arrogant and defensive about your writing, but hopefully it won't be the case. The risk is having learned to not take any nonsense from anyone for so long, at times it will be hard to tell who is well-meaning well, and who is just there to bring you down.

Now for the advantages. Older novice writers usually have more life experience to draw from, and sometimes more settings and relationships they've been through. This is good if you don't see yourself as being someone who knows everything about everything, and as a result your fiction might come across as preachy and patronizing. On the other hand, you have the wisdom of knowing better than that.

It you are a novice, older writer, but you've been an avid reader of fiction for decades, you have a huge advantage. Most young people who want to become novelists do not read enough, and it shows through their writing. They make mistakes and errors, which are a clear indications they do not spend enough time reading and not enough time studying the craft of fiction. After reading novels for a few decades, you should have a pretty solid idea of what a novel is, how it's constructed and what the techniques of fiction are—even if it's at an unconscious level. It will take you far less time to understand how to put it all together and produce relatively good work. If you have read much over the past decades, then you're pretty much ahead of a novice, young novelist.

As an older person, you might have more time, particularly if you've retired. In fact, most people who are retired have too much time on their hands, and boredom is the number one factor that makes older people depressed. All this free time can be turned productively with the writing of fiction. Young people can only dream of having such large amount free time to do some writing, but you have it, so cherish it and make the most of it.

An older person also has less financial worries if she's put enough money on the side and has paid off the mortgage. If you're only expenses are utilities and basic necessities, then you can afford to indulge in learning how to write fiction.

Being an older writer, you might come from an era or a country where grammar formed part of your education, and hence you have a good knowledge of the elements of English. This puts you in a strong position because unlike young people who haven't been taught grammar, you'll more likely to be able to edit your own work to a high-standard. If you have not learned grammar, or it's been a while, I suggest you pick up a workbook on grammar and brush up. Just like novice, young novelists, you need to learn how to walk before learning how to run.

Finally, if you do have the time and the inclination, they join a writing group or a community college class. You will not only accelerate your mastering of the craft, but you'll also make new friends who have the same interest you have, and it will also keep you motivated to persist with the learning of the craft and to finish your projects. But keep in mind about what I have said before about writing groups. If they bring you down, or you end up spending more time drinking coffee and sharing stories with members of your writing group than writing, then it might not be such a good idea.

SETTINGS

"An author knows his landscape best; he can stand around, smell the wind, get a feel for his place."

—Tony Hillerman

There are basically two types of settings—familiar and unfamiliar settings. They both have advantages and disadvantages.

Firstly, American readers in general tend to be obsessed with their own world, and hence the great majority of bestselling fiction in the USA tends to be set in America. This does not mean a novel set in another part of the world cannot become a bestselling. *The Girl with the Dragon Tattoo* series of novels is a perfect example of novels set in another country, which has attracted a huge number of readers. The Harry Potter series are all set in England, but still capture the imagination of millions of American children.

So, what's the best setting for your novels? One you're familiar with and one best suited for the story you're trying to write. Stephen King is very familiar with small town living in Maine because he lives there, and as a result he writes vivid, realistic settings of small town living. James Lee Burke's settings of the Deep South is solid, impressive and a very important part of the stories. Just like King, Burke lives in the same place as his characters, hence he is able to paint with amazing accuracy and vivid details the lives of those who live in the area.

If you live in a big city, the odds are you'll be able to write a more realistic city setting. The advantage here is you can easily research your setting by just walking around and talking to people. The same applies to small towns or any places in the world. The closer you are to the setting, the more you can absorb all its characteristics, including sounds, light, smells and so on.

Setting is one of the most important aspects of your novel, and often a good setting is as powerful as a character. A story set in the middle of New York City is going to be totally different to the same story set in the Australian outback. People are going to behave differently, the cultures will be different, the weather, the traditions, the tempers, the beliefs, the resources and so on. Let's say you've decide to write a crime novel about a serial killer. Set in New York City, the police would have enormous resources to catch the killer, including help from the FBI if requested. The same story set in the Australian outback would be totally different. The resources would be limited, the distances between locations far-and-between, the weather unbearable and taxing for all those involved, evidence easily destroyed and contaminated, bodies harder to find. You'll have a totally different story just by changing the setting.

You could select a true crime event set in another part of the world, and re-work it as a novel in a setting you are familiar with. You can change the gender of those involved as well, and suddenly you have a great blueprint to work from.

What does setting involve? First and foremost, it's the environment you experience with your five senses—sight, sound, smell, touch and taste. Everything encompassing the five senses forms a part of your environment, including place, people, objects, and mood. The closer the relationship between the environment and the characters, the better your story is likely to be. This is why James Lee Burke's novels are so compelling. The settings are so strong, they are as powerful as the characters in the stories. They impact directly on everyone's lives and on the plot. A good setting is not just there for the sake of it, but forms part of story.

When writing your novel, ask yourself if the setting you have chosen is the best one to tell your story. Could your story be better served in a different environment—a small town, a big city, another country?

The era in which your story takes place also forms part of the setting. Los Angeles in the 1920s is not going to have the same setting as Los Angeles in the 1960s or Los Angeles in the 2010s. If you are going to set your novel in a yesteryear era, then make sure you've done your research and captured the setting, culture and lifestyle of your characters accurately. With the Internet, it's fairly easy to do some research. You can also visit your local historical society for additional information and talk to elderly citizens who have lived in the area long enough to give you information not readily available in print or online.

Obviously if you are setting your novel on another planet and another time, you'll have to rely much more on your imagination than your observation skills. In this case, you are pretty free to do as you please, but the details you have in your settings should be as precise and vivid as if you were writing about a contemporary setting. In fact, with science-fiction and fantasy, you should include even more details because readers are not familiar with the environment. With contemporary settings in present time, you can skip a lot of details because people are already familiar with the setting. James Patterson uses such techniques because he sets his novels in well-known American cities like Los Angeles and New York, which everyone is familiar with through the thousands of television shows and movies set there. Just a couple of paragraphs about the settings using the fives senses is usually enough.

Whatever setting you decide to use for you novel, make sure it's appropriate to the story. If you are not sure, write the first chapter in two different settings and compare them. Which one works best? Which ones sounds truer? Which one brings forth more dramatic tension? Which one makes the characters more interesting? Which one heightens the dramatic tension?

On a final note, pages and pages of settings are no longer the norms. This was fine last century, but today the story, dialogue and characters take place first. Keep the setting detailed enough but not to a point where readers skip through all the details to get to the story.

VOICE

"For last year's words belong to last year's language. And next year's words await another voice."

—T.S. Elliot

Everything about you is unique—your face, your body, your fingerprints, your DNA, your voice, the way you think. When you write, you are projecting a 'voice'. The voice in your writing forms part of your uniqueness as a writer. When you talk, you have a unique voice. Some people project different voices when talking to different people. At work, you don't use the same language or tone you do at home or with friends. When writing fiction, the voice you use must be appropriate to the story.

Beginning novelists are uncertain about their voices. This is mainly due to not having written enough. The more you write, the more you'll find a voice you are comfortable with, one you are not forcing out, a natural voice, one created not to impress but simply to tell the story in the most effective way possible. When you talk, you do not think of the voice you are using. You just get your message across.

When you write, you should just get the story across. However, new novelists do not have a voice yet because they lack the confidence in their own voices. Instead, they try to imitate the voice and style of writers they admire—and there is nothing wrong with such technique. It's how you learn to write fiction. When you begin, you write like such-and-such, and then like such-and-such, and eventually your voice will evolve from all the readings you have done, all the writing, and your way of thinking and telling stories. Eventually, you will stop judging and comparing your voice to others. You'll be comfortable with it, in the same way you are comfortable with the car you've driven around for a couple of years, even though it might have felt 'weird' and not right at the time.

Whatever you do, do not force the voice within you. Do not write to be someone you are not when telling a story. A strong, commanding voice reassures readers you are in charge and you know what you're talking about. They trust you and are willing for you to take them on a journey.

THE SHORT STORY

"A short story is a love affair, a novel is a marriage. A short story is a photograph; a novel is a film."

—Lorrie Moore

This book is about novel writing and for the new novelist. Short stories are a genuine way to learn the craft, but they are to novels what a short film is to a feature film, or ping-pong is to tennis. The techniques are the same, but the overall approach and way to tell stories are different.

Do you need to write short stories before you write novels? No, you don't, but if you do, it's not going to hurt.

I'm personally not very good at short stories because my ideas tend to be too big to be contained in a single short story (although I have published a couple of them, one in a New York anthology, and one in a literary magazine and won an editor's favorite award). I like good character arc and stories, and short stories tend to limit the ability to tell 'bigger tales'. But they are, of course, perfect for ideas too small for longer fiction.

However, I do enjoy reading good short stories, and they can teach you a lot about the craft. It's also less daunting to work on a short story than a novel. Some short stories can be written in a single sitting, and there is some satisfaction in being able to write publishable work in such a small amount of time. With novel writing, you have to be patient and willing to work for months, sometimes years, on a story, which can be difficult when you are young because time feels much slower in your twenties than it does in your forties or fifties.

Short stories tend to focus on a single incident or a little series of incidents all inter-connected. They are not so much about plot, but more about capturing a moment, an experience, something unique for readers to experience. They tend to focus on one aspect of a character rather than an in-depth analysis of a character. They have a beginning, middle and an end (just like a short film). They use the same fiction techniques as novel writing, and it's best to show rather than tell, although you can get away with it more in short stories than in longer fiction. You 'tell' the small scenes, and you 'show' the big scenes.

For example, if a character is driving from the country to the city, but the driving is somewhat irrelevant to the story, you can simply write:

> It took her three hours to drive to the city. Once there, she decided to rent an apartment for the week.

This is 'telling' because we are not living the experience of the character through her eyes. With showing we experience everything. Re-written, the above section could begin as follows:

> She stepped inside the convertible early in the morning. The sky was clear, and the weatherman said that there would be no rain until later in the afternoon. A good day for driving. She buckled up, turned on the engine, and pulled into the traffic.

This is showing. We are experiencing through the writing what the protagonist is going through, just as if we were living it ourselves.

If the action is not important to the story, but essential or the story would be illogical, then you can just 'tell'. For any dramatic scenes, big scenes and important moments, 'show' us the action.

Keep your relationships in a short story to a minimum. You do not have the word count to introduce tens of characters and multiple sub-plots. Start with a single theme, a straightforward story line and two or three characters.

In terms of the originality of your short story, as we have seen previously with longer fiction, it's your interpretation of an idea that matters, not whether the idea has been done before or not. Bring something unique to it, be it setting, characters, gender, era, and so on. It's not different with a short story. Your vision of the story is what is going to make it unique, not whether it's an original idea or not.

Whether you are writing a novel or a short story, the same rule applies.

CONFLICT

"Conflict is drama, and how people deal with conflict shows you the kind of people they are."

—Stephen Moyer

Conflict is the essence of all drama. Without conflict, you don't have any drama. Your novel must have a major conflict in it, a main idea or situation that must be solved through conflict. I challenge you to find any worthwhile novels or movies without conflict them. It simply doesn't exist because conflict is the essence of storytelling—to place a person or persons in a situation and see if they can get out of it.

When the major conflict in the novel is resolved, it's the end of the story. There is no point in going on with a story when the major conflict you have set at the start of the novel is resolved. You've gone full circle and hopefully have left readers with a satisfying ending.

conflict at the beginning

The major conflict in your novel must appear at the start of the novel. There is no need to string along readers for two or three chapters before you set the main conflict in motion.

In my novel *Addiction* the conflict occurs in the opening chapter when Danielle finds her sister sleeping with her boyfriend. From this moment on, her life is challenged, and she must come to terms with this new reality. She loves her sister more than anyone in the world, but on the other hand, her sister is a drug addict, a liar and a narcissist, which makes the major conflict in the story pivotal to all the scenes.

In my crime novel *First Kill*, the major conflict is also set in the first chapter—a crime is committed and Katrina, our protagonist, is forced to investigate in the face of opposition. This is typical of crime novels where the protagonist is more-or-less forced to take on a case with some reluctance.

In your novel, you must establish what the main conflict is going to be and set it as early on as possible in the novel.

conflict is not violence

The world 'conflict' might give the impression violence has to be included. This is not true, although violence can form part of conflict in a novel. You are more likely to find violent conflict in a crime book, thriller or action story. Some literary novels also have violence. Conflict is simply two opposite forces coming face-to-face.

There are some talented writers, like James Lee Burke, who manage to bring forth violent conflict and intellectual conflict in one novel. Whilst James Lee Burke's protagonists tend to be fairly intelligent, at times they have to resort to violence because this is the only thing the antagonists in the stories understand. This brings forth very complex stories where both intellectual and violent conflicts work in parallel.

types of conflicts

Conflict does not have to be one person against another, although this is the most common aspect of conflicts set in stories.

In my novel *The Research*, the main conflict is between couples—what they accept or challenge as acceptable in a relationship.

Another common type of conflict is a person and herself.

In *The Suffering*, the main story is the conflict between the protagonist, Valerie, and her inability to cope with her heartbroken self.

In *Second Cut* the main conflict is between Karina and the law enforcement establishment.

Sometimes you can have the main conflict as man (or woman) versus nature. This is typical of movies like *Twister, Into the Storm* and any stories with people versus the environment.

maintaining conflict

Conflict is not people having an every day chit-chat about anything. It's not about people going about, living happy lives. This makes for poor drama and a boring novel.

One way to ensure your novel doesn't sag is to infuse conflict in every scene. Think of movies and television shows where every single scene is infused with conflict. You would be hard-pressed to find a television series without conflict in every single scene.

Whilst with novels you can get away with a little less dramatic conflict, it's best to keep the conflict on-going as much as possible in order to maintain the narrative tension.

what about happy moments?

Your characters can still be happy, make love and enjoy each other's company. However, make sure you include just enough conflict during those happy times to maintain the dramatic tension. For example, a couple might be making love, but there is noise in the background, or it's cold in the room, or one is more self-serving than the other. Or they have a slight disa-greement at the end of the lovemaking session.

Conflict and character growth

Without conflict, your protagonist cannot grow or change. A character is forced to react when faced with adversity, which is what creates the conflict in a story. When readers read a novel, they expect characters to change and learn from what is happening to them because it reflects real life. In life, we learn from our mistakes, through our conflicts with others, our environ-ment and ourselves. Make sure you give provide enough conflict for your characters to grow.

CHARACTERS

"When writing a novel a writer should create living people; people not characters. A character is a caricature."

—Ernest Hemmingway

When I was a young writer and somewhat wet behind the ears, I was given advice by one of my creative writing teachers, which I treat like gospel until this day. His advice was:
Don't make your characters more stupid than you are.
I had written a short story where the protagonist acted in ways I would have never acted had I been in his shoes. He was dumber than I was, and my writing teacher said it was too obvious I was trying to manipulate the reader.

When you create characters, you have to ensure your characters use the maxim of your own intelligence. This means you must place yourself in your characters' shoes, and based on your current level of intelligence, you have to guess what your characters would do. This means a character cannot do something stupid if you would not be doing it yourself. By following this advice, your characters will never come across as manipulated and contrived.

Your antagonists are also not idiots. They might do stupid things, but you would do the same if you had been in their situation, their culture and with their level of education. So, for example, if you are going to portray a red neck who has left school at the age of twelve, it's your job to ensure this character acts to the maxim of *your* intelligence if you were such character. This takes of a bit of imagination and sometimes some research. If you cannot empathy with others, you will find it difficult to put yourself in their shoes, and this will make it more difficult for you to create convincing characters in your fiction.

AFTERWORD

"We're past the age of heroes and hero kings. ... Most of our lives are basically mundane and dull, and it's up to the writer to find ways to make them interesting."

—John Updike

Writing is a journey into the unknown. It's a way to explore worlds we cannot always explore in real life. It's a time-consuming craft, but it's also one of the most joyful occupations you will undertake in your life. If you are spending a couple of hours a day watching television, you've got time to learn the craft of writing. In your death bed, you are not going to wish you had watched more television. You will, however, regret not writing all those books you wished you had written.

The creative writer, just like any other artist, is a warrior in a society obsessed with money. The creative person knows it is what you leave behind in life that's important—not what you accumulate.

As a new writer, or even a seasoned one who has lost touch with the craft, you need to make writing a priority because of the passion you have for it. The joy of creating stories others will read is totally unique. You can touch someone on the other side of the planet, in another country, in another world, with the power of fiction. You can inspire and change lives, the way my life has been changed by the wonderful books I have read over the years.

I've included in this volume my award-winning short story *My Father's Last Breath* so you can study freely the style and fiction techniques I have used and discussed in this book.

I hope you make your journey as a writer an exciting and fascinating one.

Kindly.

Laurent Boulanger

My Father's Last Breath

Originally published in Toasted Cheese Literary Journal, vol. 6 no. 3 in September 2006. It was selected for that month as the Editor's Pick (Billard) as Best Short Story. Part of the story is used in the novel The Girl From France, *winner of the 2014 Paris Book Festival Award for Best e-Book worldwide (five languages, all categories).*

City public hospitals are all the same. They are crowded with the sick, the wounded, the weary, doctors, nurses, specialists, cleaners, visitors and flower sellers. They smell of commercial detergent and chemicals, and nobody ever smiles unless they felt like they have an obligation to cheer someone else up. They are maze-like, and it's easy to lose oneself right at the end of the west wing when one is supposed to be at the end of the east wing, or to go up and down for a half hour just to find a toilet accessible to visitors, not just patients and hospital staff.

I'd been in and out of hospitals whenever my father's health deteriorated, but I had never attended a hospital on such a regular basis. My father usually came back home on the same day after being checked and administered the right cocktail of medication like a victim of an epileptic fit who needed to get on with life.

Hospitals scared me. They are like churches, where someone else decides the fate of other people's lives; where the sins from the past come to haunt you; where you find yourself repenting and praying to a God you have ignored for the majority of your life. In hospitals, the doctors are the gods, and the nurses are the angels.

Sometimes, while sitting in the waiting room of the critical care unit and flicking through a magazine or losing myself in Proust's *A La Recherche Des Temps Perdus*, my concentration was snapped by someone's cry of pain and despair. The shriek of another person's suffering cleaved the core of my soul like a hand to the throat. I was suddenly reminded nothing lasts forever, and life doesn't always end in the peaceful quietness of the night in the comfort of one's home amongst the familiarity of objects accumulated over a lifetime.

During my first month at the orphanage, I visited my father every Tuesday. The people at the orphanage wouldn't allow me more visits, no matter how sick my father got. There were rules and regulations written in stone over a century ago, and nobody was willing to bend them, even if the sky would suddenly fall to the earth and swallowed us all. I could beg and put on a sorry face; I could have bribed the entire establishment had I had the means to do so; but it would have made no difference whatsoever. The rules were the Ten Commandments of the orphanage, and the only ones who lived outside those rules were those who had escaped to a better world.

My father's left lung had collapsed without warning on that sunny June afternoon when our lives had radically changed. The doctor in charge of my father's convalescence at the hospital told me the technical term for a collapsed lung was tension pneumothorax, but I could refer to it as tension pneumo. Doctor talk, he confided to me as if he were my big brother. I liked him. He was in his late-twenties and good looking—different from other doctors who sported grey hair and bulging stomachs like overfed turkeys ready for the annual festive season slaughter. I was a child, but he spoke to me as if I were an adult. He never bothered to change his intonation or vocabulary to bridge our age difference or try to patronize me with his encyclopedic medical knowledge. He shared complex diagnosis and prognosis like loved ones give you a cuddle after you've run into a door left ajar.

We were sitting in his office at the hospital when he explained what had happened to my father. He used the help of a color chart pinned to the back wall, right behind his chair. The chart showed a full-frontal cross-section of the respiratory system, including the larynx, trachea, bronchi, diaphragm and lungs. Next to it was a chart of the heart in blue and red sections, showing the pathway of blood travelling from body tissues to the right atrium and to the right ventricle. I had seen similar charts pinned to the walls of the science classroom back at school and remembered the difficulty I had in memorizing all the strange names someone a long time ago had assigned to every organ and function of the body.

The doctor's name was Alfred Herrmann, and his family originated from Germany. He'd been born in Strasbourg, in the very same hospital he was now working for. He insisted I call him by his first name, which felt strange because at school we were forced to address the teachers by their surnames. Even the teachers addressed us by our surnames. I wasn't Clotilde, but Mademoiselle Benoît.

With his plastic biro, Dr. Herrmann pointed to the left lung on the color chart—the one colored blue—and said, 'See this large blood vessel?' He indicated a large artery attached to the top end of the heart.

I nodded.

'For some reason, it has burst and caused the lung to collapse in the process. As a result, your father's heart doesn't pump enough blood, and thus is incapable of delivering the required amount of oxygen to the vital tissues and organs. Your father will remain in critical care for the next few days, but we'll look after him as best as we can.'

'Is he going to live?'

'He's stable and he's being constantly monitored. His heart

is still weak from the trauma, so it's important he rests.'

'When can he go home?'

'I can't say at this stage, but I'm going to be honest with you, Clotilde, you're looking at least another two to three months in hospital, and that is in the hope his condition improves gradually without any complications.'

I sighed. How was I going to cope for that long at the orphanage by only seeing my father once a week? I missed him like a plant misses the healing rays of the sun.

Dr. Herrmann took me to the hospital canteen and bought me a lunch of salad and Swiss cheese and a chocolate mousse. I told him they didn't feed us well at the orphanage, and the food tasted horrible. I told him people were making fun of me, called me Virgin Mary, and I was scared and I wished I didn't have to be there. I wanted him to know he had to hurry up and make my father feel good again.

'I'm doing the best I can,' Dr. Herrmann said, 'but life is cruel sometimes. We're not always the ones who decide on people's fate.'

I locked my eyes with his and said, 'It's God's Will, I know.'

He didn't reply, but his face expressed surprise at my answer.

He reached for my hand and squeezed it.

I let tears roll down my face. 'I'm so tired of everything, I want a normal life again.'

'You're a brave little girl,' he finally said, 'maybe I can do something about getting you out of the orphanage. I have a friend who knows a friend who's a caseworker with the department of social security. A few phone calls, and we might be able to find you a placement with a nice family.' He smiled as if he'd just revealed the meaning of life. 'How does it sound?'

'It sounds fine,' I said because he was being nice, and I hated the idea of upsetting him.

But his offer wasn't agreeable.

I didn't want a placement with a nice family. I wanted my father back, and I wanted to go home.

*****

I shared a room with another girl, Martine, thirteen years old, long greasy dark hair down her back and a china-white complexion. Her green eyes peered out from two small slits, which looked as if they'd been cut into her flesh with a scalpel. She wore the same pair of jeans every day, jeans so tight she could hardly move, and a white, cropped cotton top, and no bra. Her little nichons were clearly visible through the T-shirt. I had no breasts to speak of, so at times I was envious, and at others I thought she was cheap. She spoke to me even though I didn't respond, because the last thing I needed was people trying to be friends with me. Most of the time I was moody and thought about nothing but my father.

I stole a packet of shaving blades from the nurse's room and tucked it on the inside cover of my pillow. I wrote everything I thought and felt in my diary. If I beat the odds and somehow managed to live to be older, I would remember what it was like to be the girl the world had rejected like a dog forced to fend for itself in a world that no longer had the heart to care for those who needed it the most.

I recorded my innermost desires.

If my father died, I wanted to die on the same day. They would bury us together in the same grave, shamefully hidden at the back of the cemetery amongst tall weeds, a site nobody visited, where the homeless, bastards and criminals were concealed from the public.

When it was known I was my father's daughter, the Catholic Church stripped him of his ministry like a judge strips a convicted criminal of his dignity. I was the burden of his shame, and I would follow him to the grave.

*****

'Martine!' I yelled.

Martine—who was sleeping next to me in a single bunk—grunted in reply. She'd been at the orphanage on-and-off for six years now. Her parents were junkies, and she'd been made a ward of the state. Every time social security found her a placement in a home, it didn't last. It was hard for her to get on with everyone, including myself. I didn't like her, but on that particular night, there was nobody else I could turn to.

I jumped from my bed. 'Martine, I think I'm dying!'

She stumbled from her metal-frame bed and flicked on the light from her side table. 'What? What have you done?'

I looked down my legs—dark blood painted my thighs and my nightgown like random brushstrokes from the doubtful hands of a painter's apprentice—and remembered the shaving blades hidden inside the cover of my pillowcase.

'I think I cut myself.' I pulled my nightgown up to my thighs. Where did the blood come from?

Martine's eyes met mine and I read cruelty in them.

'You're menstruating, *espèce de petite conne*,' she said with a smirk.

*****

'You're a woman now,' my father said. The skin on his face appeared gaunter than during my previous visits, almost translucent, and the bags under his eyes were so heavy, they might as well have been drawn with a charcoal pen.

His room at the hospital was small, but at least he didn't have to share it with anyone. A large crucifix hung above his bed head. A plastic tube was coming from under the white sheets, as well as wiring attached to an EKG monitor. All this machinery scared me. Even though I knew nothing about medical procedures, I was certain if someone still had to rely on a lot of equipment to stay alive, it meant he couldn't be doing well.

I sat on a white plastic chair next to his bed, my small hands grasping at my knees. He no longer smelled of pipe tobacco, but of freshly washed sheets and disinfectant. His hair was dull and combed to one side like a schoolboy whose mother had just cleaned him up before he had to go out into the big, dangerous world. He looked helpless—a lamb caught in a hunter's trap. This was not the father I knew and the memory of him I wanted to take back to the orphanage with me.

'There are many things I should have told you about what happens when a man and woman get together,' he said. 'It should have been your mother's job, and I didn't know how to go about it.'

'It's all right,' I said, 'Martine has told me everything.'

The expression on his face eased as if someone had just announced he would be able to go home that same afternoon. I realized he must have been counting the days backwards as to when it would have been appropriate for me to know about human reproduction, but Martine had fortuitously saved him from the burden.

I explained how Martine was my roommate, how her parents could no longer take care of her, and other family members didn't want the burden of bringing up a child who wasn't their own. I told him there had been a court case where her mother tried to retain custody of her child, but a government social worker convinced the judge she was an unfit mother who was still a junkie, and Martine was better off without her. I told him Martine had been raped at the age of twelve by a twenty-five-year-old man whom she'd became too friendly with. I told him how she wished people would understand what she'd been going through and stop treating her as if she had a mental disorder. If they could only realise she was just a victim of fate. She refused to talk to psychologists or psychiatrists because she was too proud, and doing so would have been an admission there was something wrong with her.

My father listened attentively without interrupting.

'Is she a good friend?' he asked when I had nothing more to day.

'She's just here and I'm just there.'

There was a pause, which felt like eternity. I could see the effort it took him just to breathe, and it made me sick to my stomach. I wished I was the one lying on his bed with him sitting next to me, comforting me and telling me how I was going to pull through. I didn't know what to say to him to make him feel better. He'd always been the parent, and now it was my turn. He didn't say how guilty he felt on how he'd become an affliction in my life, but the pain was clearly visible in his eyes, like that of a man who'd stopped believing in angels.

When I left the hospital I cried all the way to the orphanage.

*****

Martine and I inevitably became close friends. I turned twelve, and she made me drink two full glasses of white wine to celebrate my rite of passage to womanhood. My father usually diluted the wine with water before giving it to me at lunch or dinner. I had never drunk wine undiluted before, and the alcohol went straight to my brain. It was liquid fire blended with fruit juice, and firecrackers exploded in my head.

I shared my first cigarette with Martine and coughed through its entire length. With my second cigarette, I stopped inhaling completely, but held the smoke in my mouth for a few seconds before releasing it in the confinement of our bedroom.

We were not allowed to smoke or drink at the orphanage, but Martine had never been caught.

'If you get caught, deny everything, there's nothing they can do.' Her fishnet stockings had a hole in them, and she wore her mascara generously like Brigitte Bardot did in the sixties.

'But lying is a sin,' I protested.

'So?'

'So, you shouldn't lie.'

'If it gets me out of trouble, I lie. It's easy, nobody can tell the difference anyway. No wonder they call you Virgin Mary. Haven't you ever done anything wrong in your life?'

She kept the cigarettes and the wine locked in a large, green metal trunk under her bed. She was really clever, assertive and proud, and her defiant attitude excited me.

*****

That night when we ate dinner at the canteen, I threw up all over the table and was sent to the infirmary. My throwing-up had a domino effect, and three other kids vomited straight after seeing me emptying my stomach contents onto my plate of mash potatoes, green peas and low-grade minced meat.

'Have you been drinking?' the nurse asked, her pointy nose too close to my breath. She was young and seemed to cause no serious threat. She was almost smiling when she asked me the question.

'No,' I lied.

'Who gave you the wine?'

'I haven't been drinking.' A headache was thundering on both my temples, and I just wanted to lie down and die.

My first white lie.

Maybe they'd put me in hospital in the same room as my father's, and we'd share the same EKG monitor—two heartbeats pulsing into the one machine. Maybe they'd think my left lung was collapsing, I was suffering from some kind of hereditary illness passed on from fathers to daughters, and then they'd realise we were meant to be one forever, and it would be pointless to separate us because fate would inevitably bring us back together.

'I'll let it go for the time being,' the nurse said. 'I'll put it down as indigestion, but if you come back here drunk again, I'll have to report you.'

She gave me a tablet and sent me to my room.

Martine was right.

Lying was easy.

*****

That same night, Martine told me more about boys.

'They're only after one thing,' she said, both of us lying on my narrow, single bunk in the dark, sharing a cigarette. A lamppost outside lit the room brightly enough for us to see. The glow of the cigarette was the most visible thing, and every time one of us took a drag, the smoker's face became clear.

'What?' I took a puff, coughed and passed it on to her. I felt grown-up because I did what grow-ups told me I couldn't do.

'Your body.'

She said those two words as if it was a bad thing, but I wasn't so sure myself. At school I began to notice boys, but I never wondered if my curiosity was a bad thing or not. I knew their thinking differed from our thinking, and I was intrigued about my own body, so maybe it wasn't so strange at all. I could understand why they'd be interested in Martine's body because I was too. I wanted to look like her—to have more curves without trying, to walk with my butt wiggling, to project an air of confidence, looking as if I knew what life was all about. I wanted it badly. I didn't want to be a girl any more. I wanted to be a woman, and I wanted boys to look at me the way they looked at her.

She told me how her father forced her to have sex with him when she was nine years old, and at first I didn't believe her. She had already told me about how she was raped at the age of twelve, so how much worse could her life have been?

'He used to come at around midnight,' Martine said, lighting a new cigarette, 'when mum was asleep, her brain simmering in Valium and alcohol. The bastard crept into my room like a killer in the night. I never got to sleep before then because I knew he would be coming. He made it sound like there was nothing wrong with what we did. I didn't know at the time because I never told anyone. It just felt bad, that's all. I didn't like doing what he made me do, but he was my father, and at school they kept telling us we had to obey our parents. I thought other girls' fathers did the same to them—I thought it was what fathers did.'

I couldn't even imagine my father doing what he did to her. It wasn't even something that had crossed my mind because I had never imagined people could be horrible enough to do things to their own children.

I blew smoke into the air.

'But why?' I asked.

'Because he wanted to,' she said and took another drag.

'But why? What about your mother?'

'It wasn't the same. He liked them tight.'

'Oh,' I nodded, pretending I understood what she'd just told me.

I thought about my father at hospital. Dr. Herrmann told me he was getting better. Herrmann also told me he'd rung up a friend, the one who knew a caseworker, and they would find me a family soon. But now I was getting used to being with Martine. She was older than me, and she knew more than I did, and she told me things about life my father never told me. I liked that. It was like having a big sister.

'You want more wine?' she asked.

'Don't think so, I'm still feeling sick.'

'Ah, come on, don't be a baby.'

She poured me another glass, a cigarette butt hanging from one corner of her mouth, and we fell asleep drunk into each other's arms.

*****

On my next visit to the hospital, I wore tight Levis and a white-cropped cotton top. When I climbed the steps to the foyer, I noticed people were looking at me more than they usually would, especially the men. It didn't matter whether they were older or younger, doctors, janitors or patients, they all looked at me the same way—I was a slice of chocolate cake and they hadn't eaten for a month. I loved the attention I was getting.

I kept my chin up and walked straight across the polished floor. I didn't need to stop at reception because I knew where my father's room was. I had been visiting for three months now, once a week. It was my thirteenth visit, and the visiting felt as if it would never end. At times I wondered what my life would be like if he died. Probably not much different from now except I would visit him once a week at the cemetery instead of the hospital. I felt a lump in my throat.

In the elevator, I checked my reflection in the mirror. Martine had helped me with the make-up. I'd never worn make-up before and still had to get used to the idea. My lips were bright red—painted with blood—and my cheeks rosy like those of an alcoholic. I had Brigitte Bardot's eyes—eyelashes twice as long and thick as they were that morning. Martine said I looked sensual. I checked sensual in the dictionary and it read tending to arouse the bodily appetites, esp. the sexual appetite. That was exactly what I had been aiming at. My father said I was a woman now, and he was right. I was going to make him proud.

*****

'What on earth has got into you?' my father screamed when he saw me walk in the room. How could he scream so loud with his lung condition? The beeping on the EKG quickened like I had seen on TV when someone's gets a heart attack. He hunched himself over on the bed.

I stood there as if someone had just grabbed me by the throat and held me against the back wall of the room and was about the shred me to pieces.

'Is it this Martine girl?' he went on.

I had never seen him so angry before, thundering words at me like bullets from a gun when all I knew from him was kindness and patience. For a split second I thought about Martine's father, and how maybe there was a dark side to every man I didn't know about—even my father.

'But, Papa—'

'Look at yourself, Clotilde, you look like a slut!'

I wanted to tell him it was exactly what I wanted to look like, and who was he to tell me off since he wasn't even looking after me any more. I wanted to tell him none of this would have happened if he'd never let my mother leave us, and if he'd married her. I wanted to tell him he'd ruined all our lives by not marrying my mother, and I missed her even if I didn't remember ever being with her. Fat tears rolled down my cheeks.

'I'm sorry,' I said.

'What were you thinking, Clotilde?'

'You said I was a woman now.'

He rolled his eyes to the ceiling and forced a smile. He seemed upset by my crying.

'Come here,' he said.

I walked hesitantly towards the bed and thought about what Martine's father did to her.

He made me sit on the bed next to him. His hand reached for mine, but I couldn't take it. He wiped the tears from my face with his bony fingers and covered them in dark mascara, like black ink stains on an illustrator's skin.

'You're burning steps,' he said matter-of-factly. He pulled a tissue from a box on his side-table, wet it with his saliva, and began removing the make-up from my face. 'Don't rush through the stages of your life. This girl you're with, Martine, she's not the same as you. It's a girl who's been around the block a few times. Who knows what she's been up to.'

'But she's nice to me, she's the only one who gives a shit.'

'I'm not saying she's not a nice person, but look at the influence she has on you—even your language, listen to yourself talking.'

He pointed gently with his right hand to the crucifix above his bed to make me aware God was in the room with us.

He added, 'You're not my little Clotilde any more, are you?'

'I'm sorry, Papa, I'm only trying to do my best.'

'I know you are, and I'm sorry things have turned out the way they have.'

'I just want to go home.'

'Soon.'

I wanted to believe him with all my heart, but he looked sicker than he ever had. The veins on his temples and neck were snakes crawling out of his skin. Dr. Herrmann told me in two to three months my father would be ready to come back home. Three months had passed. Nothing had changed for the better.

'I want you to be careful out there,' my father continued. 'People are going to take advantage of you if you're not careful.'

I had nothing to be taken advantage of—no money, no home, no belongings. What could possibly be gained from taking advantage of me?

I stayed seated on the bed a little while longer, but neither of us said a word. Sadness weighted his eyes, and I couldn't help feeling I'd let him down. I wished I could just go back a few steps and be the little Clotilde he wanted me to be. I wished I'd never met Martine and her so-called 'wise ways'. But I somehow realized it was hard to step back into darkness once you'd seen the light. The world wasn't made of lollipops and pink fairy floss, but of fathers and sluts, vanishing mothers and people who mysteriously took advantage of you.

I was on a full pack of cigarettes a week when I heard the news. Dr. Herrmann said my father had put on a hell of a fight until the last minute. His right lung collapsed from doing too much work. There was nothing they could have done.

Back in July, Dr. Herrmann had told me my father was going to make it, and he didn't.

A little white lie.

And I believed him.

I was learning fast.

*****

The night Martine left the orphanage for good, I removed the shaving blades from the cover of my pillow. I didn't know what I was doing. It was dark and my eyes welled with tears. I cut my forefinger while pulling the first blade out of the plastic packaging. It didn't hurt. I placed my finger in my mouth and sucked the blood. It tasted good, like the first ray of sunrise.

I'd never seen people slash their wrists before, and I'd never read anything about it, so I cut across my left wrist. Had I cut along the main artery instead, I would have bled to death in a crimson pool, my soul united with that of my father. They would have found me in the morning, the little Virgin Mary, the 'nobody-gives-a-shit-about-you' girl, the slut, the 'little-Clotilde-bad-people-are-going-to-take-advantage-of'.

I dreamed of white wine turning red. The crucifix above my father's hospital bed bleeding where the hands and feet of Jesus had been nailed. My face covered in bright red lipstick. People throwing stones at me while I walked my way to school. People taking advantage of me.

I dreamed of being alone and everyone leaving. I dreamed

of screams no one could hear. I dreamed of my father's face distorted with pain as he tries hard to breathe the suffocating air around. I dreamed of his pipe and smelled his eau de vie, of the way my small hand felt in his, of the way he sometimes laughed when I made a joke. I dreamed of a black crow. I dreamed of Provence and Marcel Pagnol as a child. I dreamed of Marcel Proust and Jesus Christ. I dreamed of sunsets over the Cathedral of Strasbourg, of English and German tourists with cameras.

I dreamed blood.

Lots of blood.

www.ingramcontent.com/pod-product-compliance
Lightning Source LLC
Chambersburg PA
CBHW031646040426
42453CB00006B/225